GOING DEEPER

**A series of Devotional Studies
in Knowing, Loving and Serving
Our Lord Jesus Christ**

J. SIDLOW BAXTER

**ZONDERVAN
PUBLISHING HOUSE** OF THE ZONDERVAN CORPORATION
GRAND RAPIDS, MICHIGAN 49506

GOING DEEPER
Copyright by J. Sidlow Baxter

First Published U.S.A. 1959

No part to be reproduced without permission

Sixteenth printing   1978
ISBN 0-310-20641-3

Printed in the United States of America

GOING DEEPER

Other works by Dr. J. SIDLOW BAXTER

AWAKE, MY HEART

A full page of devotional Bible study for every day in the year. A special Lent and Easter section is included.

GOING DEEPER

A series of devotional studies in knowing, loving and serving our Lord Jesus Christ.

HIS PART AND OURS

Enriching exposition and devotional studies in the reciprocal union of Christ and His people.

MARK THESE MEN

Arresting studies in striking aspects of Bible characters with special relevances for our own times and the days ahead.

STUDIES IN PROBLEM TEXTS

The Word of God reaches the hearts of men by means of well-known, well-loved and well-comprehended texts but the problem texts of the Bible discipline us in patience and painstaking investigation.

EXPLORE THE BOOK

A basic, progressive, interpretative course of Bible study, in one volume, from Genesis to Revelation.

THE STRATEGIC GRASP OF THE BIBLE

An overview of Scripture.

GOD SO LOVED

An exposition of the greatest verse in the Bible.

RETHINKING OUR PRIORITIES

Words for the church, its pastor and people.

A NEW CALL TO HOLINESS

An intense look at an often neglected truth.

DEDICATION

This little book is dedicated with affectionate
esteem to my dear elder sister

MRS. MARGARET WRIGHT

always a guardian angel to me during
my childhood; an unselfish encourager in
Christian service during my youth; and
ever a prayerful follower-up of my subsequent widespread travels in the ministry
of the Word

ACKNOWLEDGMENT

How many have come under the pleasant spell of Miss Annie Johnson Flint's poems, and have found enriching comfort in them! We are grateful to the Evangelical Publishers of Toronto, Ontario, Canada, for their various attractive publications of her writings, and must here make appreciative acknowledgment of their ready permission for our use of the long excerpt on pages 89 to 92 of this book. We are only too eager to recommend our readers to obtain copies of Miss Annie Johnson Flint's poems for themselves.

FOREWORD

THERE is nothing epochal or exciting about this little volume. It does not concern itself with any keenly debated topic of the hour, and cannot hope to catch the roving eyes of those who are always looking for "some new thing". Yet it does deal with those three aspects of our relationship to Christ which are continuingly fundamental, and indeed vital, to the spiritual life of the Christian believer. Therefore the unpretentiousness of these devotional reflections does not deter us from now issuing them in printed form. So many persons have testified to spiritual help derived from other writings of ours that we now gratefully accept the "ministry of the pen" as a pleasant duty, insofar as other commitments will allow. All we hope and pray for, in sending forth this further group of messages, is that they may bring real blessing to Christian believers, and praise to our dear Saviour.

J. S. B.

CONTENTS

PART I: ABOUT KNOWING HIM

PART II: ABOUT LOVING HIM

PART III: ABOUT SERVING HIM

Part One: ABOUT KNOWING HIM

A wise philosopher has said with truth that "knowledge is power". Koheleth was equally realistic, however, when he said, "In much wisdom is much grief; and he that increaseth knowledge increaseth sorrow" (Eccles. i. 18). In this "present evil age" (Gal. i. 4) knowledge not only opens the eyes, it fills them with tears; for the more discerningly we perceive, so the more painful mystery we find underlying human life. Yet the old adage is wrong which naively avers that "where ignorance is bliss 'tis folly to be wise". Such bliss of ignorance is the "fool's paradise", which never lasts long, and "great is the fall thereof". There is a knowledge which opens the eyes to that which transcends all mere human discovery, and which at the same time comforts the heart with divine reassurance concerning the present mystery of things. Christ has come—Son of God and Saviour of men. In Him is the answer to our human sin-problem. In Him is the answer to our race's heart-cry after God and the basic truth of things. In Him is the answer to the groping and sighing of the soul after peace and joy and certainty and ultimate self-fulfilment. To know Christ as the Calvary Sin-bearer, and as the risen Saviour who personally indwells the heart, is of all knowledge the most blessed. Already He is the clear answer to many of life's most poignant problems, and He is the implicit pledge of ultimate divine answer to them all. Compared with knowing Him, all other knowledge is insignificant, incomplete, and eventually unsatisfying, as every philosopher who ever lived has realised before he died. Jesus is the Way, and the Truth, and the Life. No man cometh to the FATHER but by Him. To know Jesus as a living reality in the heart is life eternal and heaven begun below.

THE BEST AMBITION

"That I may know Him, and the power of His resurrection, and the fellowship of His sufferings, being made conformable unto His death."—Phil. iii. 10.

CAN God be certainly and directly known by us? We are thinking cautiously and reflectively when we reply: Outside of Christ and the Bible, No. Can we find Him through philosophy, or science, or the non-biblical religions? No. After millenniums of groping, human philosophy offers nothing beyond unfinalised speculations. Science, whether it weighs the stars or splits the atom, comes to a dead end whenever it touches the line between the material and the spiritual. The non-biblical religions, even allowing for all that is best in them, express merely the quest, not the realised goal. Even the most hoary of them can only say, "We seek." None can say, "We have found."

Yet God *may* be truly and experientially known through the Lord Jesus Christ, who is none other than the eternal Word become flesh, the very Deity incarnate in our humanity, the "Lamb slain from the foundation of the world", the only but all-sufficient Redeemer, Reconciler, and Restorer of men to God. In Him alone, but in Him directly and heart-satisfyingly, we may know the Creator-Spirit of the universe, and hold fellowship with Him as our heavenly Father. Did not our Lord Jesus say, "I am the way, the truth, and the life: no man cometh unto the Father but by Me"? Did He not later add, "He that hath seen Me hath seen the Father"? Did He not afterward declare, "This is life eternal, that they might know Thee the only true God, and Jesus Christ whom Thou hast sent"?

Nothing can be more sacred or vital or wonderful, therefore, than to know the Lord Jesus Christ Himself, as Paul longed increasingly to know Him when he wrote, "That I may know Him, and the power of His resurrection, and the fellowship of His sufferings, being made conformable unto His death." Nor can

we over-emphasise the necessary prerequisite of clearly understanding what is *meant* by knowing Christ in that way.

Four Ways of Knowing

There are four ways of knowing a person. We may know someone merely *historically*, by records which have been preserved.
In that way we may know many great figures of the past: Moses,
Samuel, David, Daniel, Socrates, Julius Caesar, Herod, Augustine, Napoleon, and others who have commanded more than
ordinary attention on the stage of history.

We may also know a person *contemporaneously*. He, or she,
synchronises with our own day and generation. If that person
is a man, we know him, not merely as he *was*, but as he now *is*
to us in the present. At this moment, as I express these thoughts,
Sir Winston Churchill is a thriving octogenarian. I have read
and learned so much about him that I could almost think I had
met him. Certainly I know far more about him than I could
ever know about celebrities of the past. Yet even so, I cannot
say that I know him directly, by personal introduction and
contact.

Then again, we may know a person *contactually*. This, of
course, is much closer than merely knowing "about" someone;
yet it may mean no more than chance or casual contacts. There
are those whom we meet now and then in social life or in business connections. We pass the "time of day" with them, interchange comments on current topics, happen to know that they
are married, or are not married, that they are this or that or
the other; but that is about all; we do not know them closely,
or as "bosom friends".

But there are those whom we know *familiarly*. We know them
both by name and nature. We are frequently or even continually
in their presence. We know them mind-to-mind; their characteristic ways of thinking, feeling, reacting; their disposition, temperament, habits, idiosyncrasies. There is close friendship and
fellowship, or even heart-to-heart love between us and them.

Even so, there are the same four ways of knowing Christ. We
may know Him merely *historically*, believing that He really
lived, died, rose, and ascended, exactly as the Gospel narratives

tell; believing that He really was the Son of God, the supreme Exemplar, the Saviour of the world; believing it all, yet only in the sense of assenting with the mind, and not in the deeper sense of accepting with the heart.

Or we may know Him *contemporaneously*, believing in Him as the risen One who said, "Lo, I am with you all the days, even to the end of the age", yet not knowing Him by direct contact.

We may even know Him *contactually*, having received Him spiritually to indwell us as our Saviour, and yet not know Him in the way that Paul meant when he said, "That I may know Him, and the power of His resurrection, and the fellowship of His sufferings, being made conformable unto His death."

Paul wanted to know His heavenly Lord with a reverent, holy *familiarity*, in a continually deeper, richer, spirit-to-spirit communion with Him; in an ever-expanding experiential exploration; and he expresses this in writing so that we ourselves may have the same reverent heart-longing toward Christ. This indeed should be the focus-point of all Christian desire: *"That I may know HIM."*

Should We not Long to Know Him?

How *understandable* it is that we should long to know Him! Would it not be passing strange if it were otherwise, considering all He has done for us, and all He has become to us, and all He is in Himself?

Away back in the grim old days of slavery, see that emaciated negro as he waits trembling in a slave market. Soon he is sold to the hardest slave-owner who ever curled a whip over the bodies of his cringing victims. The servitude is almost unendurably rigorous; the chastisements for default are merciless; the plight of the wretched slave and his fellows is pitiful. One night he attempts escape, but is dragged back, whereupon his gloating owner decides to inflict exemplary punishment—a major lashing such as almost always means death to the undernourished slaves. In the morning he is tied naked to the whipping-post; the whippers are called; and he is just about to be thrashed before onlooking slaves and several white visitors, when a strange thing happens. One of the visitors, a tall, noble-looking gentleman, exclaims,

"Stay; you cannot whip that poor slave so brutally; he will die!"
The slave-owner, little dreaming what is to follow, glares and
retorts, "Then die he shall, unless *you*, brave sir, will take his
punishment." The handsome stranger steps forward. "You have
committed yourself," he says to the wicked owner. "Free the
slave, and *I* will take the lashing." He bares his back to the
smiters; his body quivers under the lashes; but he endures man-
fully until the last two strokes, when he sinks to the ground,
lacerated, bleeding, exhausted.

There is more to follow, however. Imagine our slave's increasing astonishment when, some days later, he is summoned
before his master, who says, "You are my slave no longer. That
man who suffered for you has now paid such a price to free you
that I cannot keep you any longer. Go. You are free."

Nor is even that all; for on going out the freed slave is intercepted by a messenger from his amazing benefactor, with new
clothing and good food, and a message that all the money he can
require has been deposited for him at a central bank.

But the climax comes when, on enquiring at the bank, he
learns the name of his wonderful deliverer and succourer. He is
a king's son; is incalculably rich; is the freer of many, many
other suffering slaves; is so upright and noble, so strong yet so
humble, so unselfish, gracious and kindly, so understanding and
individually sympathetic, that all his great household love him,
and find him ever more lovable the more they know him.

Well, is it surprising that the consuming passion of our liberated
slave is now to traverse the hundreds of miles, whatever the
hazards may be, if only he may get to his benign benefactor, fall
at his feet, look up into his face, become his willing bondservant,
then enjoy knowing him, loving him, and serving him for ever?
Is it surprising that he wants to be ever in his noble rescuer's
presence, looking into that wise, kind, gracious countenance,
knowing him face-to-face, and even heart-to-heart?

Does my little parable seem far-fetched or over-drawn? Nay,
it simply cannot be; for the reality which it pictures utterly
exceeds all possible analogies or illustrations. That wretched
slave, do I not recognise him? Do I not see myself in him, under
that worst of all tyrants, Sin? And as I reflect on the *eternal*
ruin involved in *my* slavery, do I not see my own plight as far

worse than his? Is not that noble benefactor who suffered in the
slave's place, and bought his freedom, and provided for his needs,
and became so dear to him, my own divine Saviour, the Prince
of Glory, the Lord Jesus, only that the comparison seems poverty-
stricken over against *His* infinitely greater and costlier interposition to redeem and eternally enrich *me?* Is it to be wondered at,
if now my consuming ambition becomes, *"That I may know
Him . . ."?* Is it surprising if all of us who thus know Him as
our infinite-minded, gracious-hearted, divine-human Redeemer
and Friend now long to know Him better and better, by a continually growing exploration of His boundless nature and glorious
love? Would it not be strange if it were otherwise?

But Can We Know Him Directly?

But then *can* we know Christ directly? We have been assuming that we can, but is such assumption merely gratuitous
credulity or fond delusion? Doubtless the apostle Paul meant
knowing Him thus, as we have said, for he uses a Greek verb-
form here which implies it. Yet as soon as we pause to think
of it, this is quite astounding. When Paul said, "That I may
know Him", he was speaking of Someone who had already lived
and died and passed beyond, and whom he had never met or even
seen on earth. How then could he now converse and develop
friendship with such a departed One? Still more may it be asked
how can *we,* who live two thousand years later, establish inter-
communication with Him?

Many of us think a great deal about John and Peter, Augustine
and Calvin, Wesley and Whitefield; we know much about them;
but we cannot contact them or know them personally, for they
are long since buried and departed. Nor can any Buddhist or
Mohammedan know Buddha or Mohammed by direct contact
today. Nay, the very suggestion would be ridiculed as absurd
by their devotees; for like all other mortals, Buddha and Mohammed succumbed to death, and their spirits fled from this earthly
scene centuries ago. How then could Paul, or how can we ourselves, know Jesus personally and continuingly?

It is because HE IS ALIVE.

But stay; if we believe in an after-life at all, do we not believe
that *all* the departed are alive? Yes, we do; but *they* are not

alive in the same way as our Lord Jesus. There are certain ways in which *He* is alive which belong *only* to Him, making Him a unique and communicable present-day reality.

First, He is alive *bodily*. No other departed human spirit is. Over all others the grave is victor, and they, at present, are its bodiless victims. Jesus is risen bodily, in token that He has *conquered* death, which means, among other things, that death cannot obstruct His communicating with us from the realm of the departed, even in His human nature, if He so wills. He is risen bodily, which also gives proof that He continues to live personally and humanly: there is no disintegration of personality, and no vaporising away of His real humanity. In Luke xxiv. 15 there is lovely significance in the little reflexive pronoun, "himself". Luke says, "And it came to pass that while they communed together and reasoned, Jesus *Himself* drew near, and went with them." Mark it well: it was "Jesus *Himself*", the very same Jesus, unchanged after His death and burial and resurrection, except that He now had that wonderful resurrection-body which death can never destroy. Yes, He is alive bodily, personally, humanly, the very same Jesus whom we see moving before us in the pages of the four Gospels.

Second, He is alive *regnantly*. He not only conquered death physically; He reigns over death and hades in the spirit-realm. When He first appeared to the apostle John on the Isle of Patmos, His introductory declaration was, "I am He that liveth, and became dead; and, behold, I am alive for evermore, Amen; *and I have the keys of hades and of death*" (Rev. i. 18). So Jesus is both bodily and spiritually alive, with absolute power over all the spheres and intelligences of that invisible realm!

Third, He is alive *actively*. All the millions of other human beings who have preceded us in human history are not only passed into the Beyond, they are removed from any further active participation in the affairs of this present life on earth; but Jesus is continuingly and ever-actively contemporaneous. He is neither an empty echo of the past nor a mere vague shadow haunting the present. He personally participates and actively intervenes in this modern age of ours, and in our lives as individuals. Buddha does not and cannot, nor can Confucius, nor can Mohammed, nor can any of the misty Hindu sages; but our Lord Jesus *does*. Recall that parting word which ends Mark's Gospel: "So then after the

Lord had spoken unto them, He was received up into heaven, and sat on the right hand of God. And they (the disciples) went forth, and preached everywhere, *the Lord working with them. . . ."* His followers did not lose Him when He left them. Nay, the lovely paradox is that He never more truly came to us than when He went away; for when He disappeared from local visibility He thereby came back in larger activities, spiritually and invisibly, as we see all through the Acts of the Apostles. Indeed, that well-tested and authenticated record which we call the Acts of the Apostles is so full of the invisible Lord's operations through His Spirit-filled disciples that some expositors insist on naming the book "The Acts of the Ascended Christ".

Fourth, He is alive *omnipresently*. But was He not *always* omnipresent as the pre-incarnate divine Son? Yes, but He was not then omnipresent as *Jesus*. He was, as He evermore is, the eternal Son of God, and God the Son, but He was not the Son of Man until He was born of Mary. He has now become Man by a real human birth; He has lived our life, and shared our lot, and undergone our temptations, and borne our griefs, and died our death; and He has risen again, still the same Jesus, for He is "Jesus Christ the same yesterday and today and to the ages" (Heb. xiii. 8). His human nature (marvel again at the miracle and mystery of it!) is now blended *for ever* with His deity; and He is now omnipresently with *all* His people everywhere, and with *each* of us, as the ever-living, ever-loving Lord JESUS. Listen again to His globe-encircling promise, "Where two or three are gathered together in My Name, there am I in the midst of them" (Matt. xviii. 20). Yes, He is with us omnipresently as JESUS.

Perhaps it is only amplifying what we have just said if we add that He is alive and with us *ever-abidingly*. There is a form of æsthetic admiration which says, "Leave Jesus just where history gave Him to us. We do not want the Christ of your argumentative theologies. Leave us the *real* Jesus of history, with the Judæan hills and Galilean towns as the background, and the picturesque scenes of that old-time Palestine around Him. He is most beautiful *there*, where He really belongs." But the fact is, you *cannot* leave Him there, any more than you can leave Him in the grave. He comes to you in resurrection splendour and announces, *"Lo, I am with you all the days, even unto the end of the age."* You cannot put Him under some beautiful glass case, or frame Him in some beautiful picture, as you do with other notable figures in the galleries of fame. He steps right out of the past into the living present, and walks ever-abidingly with His people to the farthest vista of the future.

And He is with us *savingly*. He graciously interferes in individual human lives, startling, wooing, challenging, rescuing, converting, reclaiming, renewing, restoring, transforming. "He is able to save to the uttermost . . . seeing He ever liveth . . ." (Heb. vii. 25).

Yes, this incomparable Lord Jesus is alive bodily, regnantly, actively, omnipresently, ever-abidingly, and savingly; but even that is not all. He is alive *anticipatively*. He not only comes to us from the past, and companions us in the present, He breaks upon us even from the future! Did He not Himself say, "And if I go and prepare a place for you, *I will come again*, and receive you unto Myself, that where I am, there ye may be also" (John xiv. 3)? And does not the Bible end with His "Surely, I come quickly"?

Oh, this wonderful Saviour-Friend! *That* is why we can know Him, and converse with Him, and be guided by Him, and develop a heart-to-heart fellowship with Him today. HE IS RISEN AND VITALLY PRESENT AS OUR LORD AND SAVIOUR JESUS CHRIST, the very One who meets us in the four Gospel memoirs, full of divine compassion and human sympathy; gracious to heal, and mighty to save!

Three Preliminaries

So, then, we may really know our Lord Jesus today in the way Paul meant when he said, "That I may know Him." Look again, therefore, at his words, and be confirmed in three simple preliminaries.

(1) As we have before said, Paul obviously means us to be in communication with Christ *directly*. Consider well the pronoun: "That I may know *HIM*". We are to know *"HIM"*; not merely the Christ of the creeds or the Jesus of tradition, but *"HIM"*; not just as One who is interpreted to us through sermons or books or even in the Bible, but *"HIM"*; not merely theoretically or sentimentally, but experientially, *"HIM"*.

(2) To "know Him" must be our *controlling desire* as Christian believers, even as it was with Paul. He cannot be known just by hurried snatches of two-or-three-minute "prayers" in a morning or at bed-time. We must somehow get unhurriedly alone with Him long enough and often enough for Him to fulfil that promise of John xiv. 21, "He that loveth Me shall be loved of my Father; and I will love Him, and will manifest Myself to Him." To know Him thus must be our dearest and deepest ambition. Think how men have been mastered by the passion for money, the passion for power, the passion for knowledge, the passion to discover, to invent, to achieve. Then reflect how pathetically lackadaisical most of us are in this holiest and heavenliest pursuit of all! How easily we give way to discouragements and interruptions! There is a place for human *resolving* in this matter of knowing Christ. Spasmodic outbursts of prayer can never take the place of regular, daily withdrawings into His presence. It is as Hosea vi. 3 tells us: "*Then* shall we *know*, if we *follow on* to know the Lord. . . ."

(3) The words, "That I may know Him", evidently indicate a *developing* communion with Christ. Paul already knew Christ in life-transforming experience, but he could not halt there. Vivid and thrilling though it was, it was the starting-point, not the goal. In communion with such a Christ there could be nothing static or final. Here was the ocean without shore, the continent without bounds. His words mean, "That I may *increasingly* know Him". By way of illustration, even though the illustration is necessarily inadequate, think of two noble-minded lovers. Their hearts are fully open to each other. There is not a thing they would withhold from each other. They have come to know each other better than they know anyone else in the world. Do they therefore say, "We now know each other fully. There we must stop. Further fellowship is futile"? Certainly not! They know that human personality is an endless treasure-mine, and that there are breadths and lengths and depths and heights which can only be discovered and mutually enjoyed by continuing love and sharing. Much more so is it between the believer and our divine Saviour. As Colossians ii. 3 says, "In Him are hid all the treasures of wisdom and knowledge." But mark: the treasures are not only *in* Him; they are "*hid*" in Him. Why are they "hid"? Is it because of reluctance to reveal them? No, it is so that you and I may have *the joy of continual discovery*!—if we

will make time to "know Him". Oh, to pray more! Oh, to know Him better! Oh, to discover those best of all treasures! We sometimes sing,

> There are depths of love that I cannot know
> Till I cross the narrow sea.
> There are heights of joy that I may not reach
> Till I rest in heaven with Thee.

But as we sing those lines do we accept them with a misguided resignation? Do we not far too lazily postpone some of those "depths" and "heights" to the other side of the grave? Would it not be equally true to change the wording a little, and sing the verse as follows?—

> There are depths of love that I *ought* to know
> Ere I cross the narrow sea.
> There are heights of joy that I *ought* to reach
> Ere I rest in heaven with Thee.

When I was a little boy, my dear mother used to take me to the Methodist "class meetings" in our area. I was too young to grasp much of what was said, but I remember one brother who always prayed, "Lord, make us all that redeemed sinners can become, *this side of heaven.*" It is a prayer we all may well pray; for although salvation is by grace alone, will not our *character* in the Beyond be affected by what we are on "*this side*"?

Is it not time for some of us to be saying with the bride in the Song of Solomon, "I will seek Him whom my soul loveth"? Only a short time after that, she was able to say, "I *found* Him whom my soul loveth." So shall it be with us, if we truly seek Him. We shall find Him, to our heart's delight. If with Paul we make our dearest purpose, "That I may know Him", it will not be long before we find ourselves singing *another* verse of the hymn we have just quoted, and singing it with new gratitude—

> Oh, the pure delight of a single hour
> Which before Thy throne I spend;
> When I kneel in prayer, and with Thee, my Lord,
> *I commune as friend with friend!*

THE FOCUS-POINT

Many persons flatter themselves that they are going to be saved because they know a great deal *about* Jesus Christ. But mere knowledge *about* Him will not save. Noah's carpenters probably knew as much about the ark as Noah did, and perhaps more. They knew that the ark was strong; they knew that it was built to stand the deluge; they knew that it was made to float upon the waters; they had helped to build it. Yet they were just as helpless when the flood came as men who lived thousands of miles away.

D. L. Moody.

THE FOCUS-POINT

"That I may know Him . . ."—Phil. iii. 10.

THIS clause, "That I may know Him", concentrates to a focus-point the master passion of Paul the spiritual explorer. Moreover, as the context indicates, the aspiring apostle would have us fall in line behind him as our eager exemplar. See especially verse 17: "Brethren, be followers together of me." In this loveliest of all senses, then, should not you and I devoutly resolve to be in the "apostolic succession"? We should, and if we have that in view, we find Paul's flaming aspiration lighting up the way for us with torch-like blaze.

"That I may know Him." Think of Paul's fervent quest in three ways: (1) what lies behind it; (2) what glows within it; (3) what gleams beyond it. At the same time, see how it allures and guides us to a similarly sanctifying, ever-developing exploration of Christ.

What Lies Behind It

We all realise, of course, that when Paul wrote the words, "That I may know Him", he was not wistfully sighing to become acquainted with Someone whom as yet he did *not* know. Nay, the fact is that he had now known Christ in soul-saving union for approximately thirty years, and was a spiritually mature believer.

We ought to mark well this fact, that away back there on the Damascus road, three decades earlier, Paul had come to know Christ by *supernatural revelation*. That is how he himself explains it. In Galatians i. 15, 16, he says, "When it pleased God . . . who called me by His grace, *to reveal His Son in me*. . . ." There is a whole world of meaning in that, for you and me today.

Although Christ was really born into our humanity by that Bethlehem miracle of two millenniums ago; although He really lived, taught, wrought, died for our sins, rose from the grave,

25

and ascended to heaven; although He is now continuingly alive in the invisible realm, bodily, regnantly, actively, omnipresently; and although all this has now been permanently fixed for us in the supernaturally inspired literature of our New Testament—recorded in the Gospels, and interpreted in the epistles; yet even that historical and doctrinal revelation does not become an inward, saving, spiritual reality to any individual until the Holy Spirit illumines the mind. A man may read it, and know it, and assent to it in full, yet not really "know" it at all with an inward, regenerating luminousness. The "revelation" itself must be revealed! What though the sun is shining at meridian splendour if the man on whom it is shining is blind? The outward, objective revelation is real enough; but it requires as its counterpart an inward subjective illumination.

Our Lord Himself teaches that He can only be known through this inward, divine clarification. See Matthew xi. 25–27: "At that time Jesus answered and said, I thank Thee, O Father, Lord of heaven and earth, because Thou hast hid these things from the wise and prudent, and hast *revealed them unto babes.* . . . No man knoweth the Son but the Father; neither knoweth any man the Father, save the Son, and he to whomsoever the Son will reveal Him." The arresting thing in that pronouncement is not so much that no man knows the Father except through the Son, but that "no man knoweth the *Son*" except those "babes" to whom the *Father* reveals Him. The revealing Son must Himself be revealed; and He can be revealed only to "babes". Why? Because few can become "wise and prudent", whereas all may become "babes" if they will.

At the end of His Galilean itinerary our Lord asked the disciples, "Whom say ye that I am?" When Peter answered, "Thou art the Christ, the Son of the living God", our Lord commented, "Blessed art thou, Simon, son of Jonas; for flesh and blood hath not revealed it unto thee, but my Father which is in heaven" (Matt. xvi. 15–17). That was after about one year and ten months circuiting of Galilee, living with Jesus continually, observing Him in public and in private, hearing all the discourses, seeing all the miracles, watching Him under all circumstances and on all occasions, and witnessing all the accumulating credentials of His divinity. Yet even then Peter's inward perceiving of our Lord as the Son of God was the result, not so much of mental deduction, as of spiritual disclosure from above.

Well, that was how Paul, too, began: "When it pleased God . . . to *reveal His Son in me*. . . ." That is how each of us today must needs come to "know Him" in a true, spiritual, person-to-person way. "Eye hath not seen, nor ear heard, neither have entered into the heart of man, the things which God hath prepared for them that love Him. But God hath *revealed them unto us by His Spirit*. . . . We have received the Spirit of God, that we might *know* . . ." (1 Cor. ii. 9–12).

This, of course, lays our natural pride of learning in the dust. Perhaps some of us have liked to think that we ourselves have made at least a part-contribution; but we have been wrong. In whatever degree we really know Christ, it is of divine revelation. By our own reading and reasoning we may know much about Him as the Jesus of Scripture, the Messiah of Israel, the Prophet of Galilee, the ideal human character, the Saviour of the race; but to know Him personally, who is the divine Son, is a matter of inward revelation. It is something out of the realm of "flesh and blood", and beyond the area of natural reasoning. "The natural man receiveth not the things of the Spirit of God . . . because they are spiritually discerned." "But he that is spiritual discerneth all things" (1 Cor. ii. 14, 15).

How sure some of the people in our Lord's day were that *they* knew Him! See how precisely the men of Nazareth pin-point His identity: "Is not this the carpenter's son? Is not his mother called Mary? And his brethren, James and Joses and Simon and Judas, and his sisters, are they not all with us?" (Matt. xiii. 55, 56). See how easily the various groups recognise Him: "Some say that Thou art John the Baptist; some Elijah; and others Jeremiah, or one of the prophets" (Matt. xvi. 14). Looking back on it all, more than fifty years later, John writes, "He was in the world, and the world was made by Him, and the world *knew Him not*" (John. i. 10). Why, even the King's herald, John the Baptist, did not know Him with opened eyes until he saw *inwardly* something that happened *outwardly*: "And I knew Him not; but He that sent me to baptise with water, the same said unto me, Upon whom thou shalt see the Spirit descending, and remaining on Him, the same is He which baptiseth with the Holy

Spirit. *And I saw* and bare record that this is the Son of God"
(John. i. 34).

Is there then no place for logical evidence, scientific evaluation,
or the exercise of reason, in relation to knowing Christ? In one
sense, Yes; in the spiritual sense, No. Logical evidences and
reasoned arguments can remove the stumbling-stones which im-
pede the way to faith. The exercise of reason upon the well-
authenticated facts of Christianity can convince the mind, and
prepare the heart to receive Christ, and influence the will to make
active decision toward Him; but human intellect absolutely *cannot* take us any *further* than that. At that point God Himself
must make Christ real to us, or we cannot spiritually "know
Him".

Perhaps someone here objects: If Christ can only be known
truly and spiritually by those to whom the Father reveals Him,
does not that reduce our human side of the matter to a negative
passivity? What is the good of even *trying* to know Him, since
we can accomplish simply nothing until the Father moves in our
direction? What is the point of preaching a "whosoever will may
come" Gospel, or of exhorting men indiscriminately to know
Christ, when the fact is that they are helplessly unable, unless
the Father by His Spirit *moves* upon them, and *reveals* Christ to
them? Are we not back at the old hyper-Calvinist position of
"human inability"?

To that objection our answer is unhesitating. It confuses (as
hyper-Calvinist writers always have done) so-called "moral inability" with *spiritual* incapacity. It implies that because fallen
man is *spiritually* incapacitated, he does not have even the *moral*
ability to respond to the Gospel, and must therefore remain idly
passive until the divine Spirit sovereignly moves upon him. To
our own mind, that hyper-Calvinist idea carries a pious libel on
the character of God; for to say that God proclaims His love
to "the whole world", and provides His only-begotten Son
as "the Lamb of God which taketh away the sin of the world",
and publishes a "whosoever will" invitation to all men, while
all the time He pre-decides that only a certain few shall be
saved, and all the rest in their millions shall be coldly left
in utter inability to respond, even if they would, reduces the
Bible doctrine of redemption to a vast scheme of theatrical
hypocrisy.

The vital thing to realise is, that although fallen man is *spiritually* "dead", he nevertheless *does* have still in his nature the *mental and moral* ability to appreciate, to accept, and to believe divine truth. He cannot regenerate himself; but he *can* intelligently understand the plain message of the Gospel; he *can* appreciate the reasonableness and graciousness of it; he *can* feel a conscience-stricken sense of need for Christ; he *can* respond gratefully and penitently to it in mind and heart; and he *can* allow himself to be drawn by it into seeking Christ. Even the last-mentioned does not spiritually regenerate him, but (mark it well) all these things a man *can* do, that is, he has the mental and moral "ability" to do, even while he is still spiritually un-regenerate. To deny this is to say that man has less "moral ability" toward the Gospel than toward anything else. Fallen man *does* have the "moral ability" to respond to the Gospel, despite his *spiritual* incapacitatedness; and when an unconverted man does indeed thus respond sincerely to the Gospel, the Holy Spirit has His opportunity; He infuses that vital inspiration which creates appropriating faith, regenerates the human spirit, and illumines the human mind with spiritual truth.

Now all this may seem to be a veering away from the simple directness of Paul's words, "That I may know Him"; yet we are persuaded that for some of us, at least, our detour has been necessary, if only to emphasise that to know Christ in a true and spiritual way there must be this inward revelation or illumination of which we have been speaking. We should be sorry to think that we were making the knowing of Christ seem a complicated or mysterious matter. Let us sum up what we have said, and then come right back again to our text.

(1) Our Lord Jesus is real, is alive, is present, and may be directly known by us.

(2) If we are truly to know Him and commune with Him, we need that the Holy Spirit shall reveal Him.

(3) Therefore we must come humbly, with all pride of self-ability to know laid low, in reverent dependence on the revealing Spirit.

(4) If we thus "seek" we shall certainly "find", for wherever there is such outgoing of heart toward Christ, inward revelation by the Holy Spirit rewards it, and creates further spiritual capacity to know.

Of course, most of us who are now reflecting on this subject have already experienced in some degree the reality of this inward revelation by which Christ is known. We have become united to Christ by a real conversion, and can say with Paul, "It pleased God . . . to reveal His Son in *me*." Our holy ambition now must be to *go on* in Spirit-illuminated exploration; and we may confidently look to God, saying with the psalmist, "In *Thy* light shall we *see* light" (Ps. xxxvi. 9).

The very thing which lays our natural pride of knowledge in the dust—"No man knoweth the Son but the Father", is that which also beckons us on most tenderly and reassuringly—"Thou hast hid these things from the wise and prudent, and hast revealed them unto babes". To all the humble-hearted and spiritual-minded, Heaven says, "Ask, and it shall be given you. Seek, and ye shall find. Knock, and it shall be opened unto you" (Matt. vii. 7).

What Glows Within It

Now as soon as we remember those thirty years of Christian experience which lay behind Paul's words, "That I may know Him", we begin to sense how rich and mutual his fellowship with Christ must have been. Such had it been indeed that his whole soul now cried out with mingling rapture and hunger to know more and more of that pure heaven which lives in the boundless bosom of God's dear Son.

> Since I Thy love have known,
> Nought else can satisfy;
> The fulness of Thy love alone,
> For this, for this, I cry.

All his discoveries had only made him see how much *more* there was to discover. This was a glorious sea with ever-wider horizons the further one sailed into it. This was a sun-flooded mountain with ever-lovelier up-reaches the higher one climbed it.

This was a boundless continent with ever-richer expanses the more one explored it.

We often say that Columbus discovered America. In one sense that is true enough, but in another it is *far* from the truth. America is *still* being discovered. In northern Canada alone there are one thousand still-unnamed lakes! And even in the quickly populating south of the United States, all kinds of new riches are even now being discovered beneath the soil.

It is even so with our knowing of Christ. Conversion is a start, not a goal. When we slump into thinking of the Christian life as static we are in spiritual decline and peril. When we put limits to Christ, our organ of vision is diseased. Even when we say with Paul, "That I may know Him", we must never let the sentence end there. It must always be, "That I may know Him, *and* . . ." The universe invites us. Having conquered the land by wheels, we must ride the seas in ships, then fly the skies with wings, then reach beyond into the spaces, to the moon and the planets. That is exactly the quest of the natural man in relation to the physical universe; and it must be so with the spiritual man in relation to that living, incarnate universe of divine love, our Lord Jesus. There is to be a continually enlarging mental apprehension and spiritual appropriation of Christ. Oh, fellow-Christian, if only you and I may see vividly enough that all this really lies before us, will it not make prayer-communion with Christ the *supreme* thing with us?

Perhaps Paul himself as a character-study most aptly illustrates this ever-expanding mental and spiritual concept of Christ. First of all he regarded Jesus as a self-deluded pseudo-Messiah who had justly suffered crucifixion for blasphemy. Then in the spiritual earthquake of his experience on the Damascus Road, he had learned to his astonishment that the Jesus whom he was so madly fighting *was* the Messiah, Israel's long-expected *true* Messiah. Doubtless, even then, at first, his views of Jesus as the Messiah would be constricted by the general ideas which then prevailed on the subject among the Jews—and they were pretty cramped, Judaistic, earthly, temporal, as we glean from the four Gospels.

But soon, now, Paul came to see in Jesus a far bigger Christ or Messiah than one who was simply to exalt Israel with material advantages. This meek and lowly, risen and reigning Lord Jesus was a cosmic Christ with racial significances transcending all merely global or temporal measurements. He was the Son of God as well as the Son of David. He was the world's Saviour as well as Israel's Messiah. He had not only fulfilled all the Old Testament forecasts, but had immeasurably transcended them. The inspired Hebrew prophets had pre-envisaged a Davidic, Messianic kingdom and empire in which Israel should be the centre, with all other peoples of the earth included and blessed. But Jesus is God-Man Christ and Saviour who is "before all things", and in whom "all things cohere", visible and invisible, on earth and in the heavens, a Christ who is the Centre-Mind of the whole colossal universe, in whom Satanic, angelic, and human sin was bound to find its central target, and whose Cross has a reconciling reach throughout all the immense areas of created existence (Col. i. 20).

Indeed, Paul's Christ now becomes lifted right out from all geographical and historical confinements. "Though we have known Christ after the flesh, yet now henceforth know we Him (thus) no more" (2 Cor. v. 16). The Cross is no longer the event of a mere time-date, but the making "manifest" in history of that which was in the heart of God "before the ages of time" (2 Tim. i. 9; Titus i. 1). And our Lord Jesus Himself becomes not only the Christ of time-dispensations but of the divine purpose which runs right through the pre-time, mid-time, and post-time "ages" (Eph. i. 4, 5, 10; iii. 11). Time itself is a mere parenthesis. It cannot contain this illimitable Christ. He belongs to the infinities and eternities. He grows bigger and bigger. He goes farther and farther. Yet he loses none of His real, divine-human personality, individuality, sympathy; and the lovely paradox is that the bigger and higher and further He seems, the nearer and clearer and dearer He becomes to the prayerful human heart, until Paul can only exclaim again from pure joy and hunger, *"that I may know him . . ."*

> Yea, fill to overflow,
> Naught less enough for me;
> Till other hearts through mine shall know
> The heaven of joy in Thee.

What Gleams Beyond It

Even his most eager anticipation of *heaven* was expressing it-self when Paul wrote, "That I may know Him . . ." The undying rapture of paradise itself would consist in knowing Him in an ever-unfolding revelation and enjoyment. Paul meant his readers to understand that this would be the cry on his lips as he passed out into the Beyond—"That I may know Him . . ." There, in that ampler, sublimer life, amid a perfectly conducive environment, with expanded capacities of apprehension, and the conferment of superior capabilities, his never-ending heaven of heavens would be the progressive enjoyment of a human-hearted but divine Christ becoming ever more glorious and rewarding through ten million ages. "For now (by comparison) we see through a glass, darkly; but then face to face. Now I know in part; but then shall I know even as I am known" (I Cor. xiii. 12). "To me to live is Christ, and to die is gain . . . to be with Christ which is far better" (Phil. i. 21–23).

> O Christ, Thou art the Fountain,
>   The deep, sweet well of love;
> The streams on earth I've tasted;
>   More deep I'll drink above.
> There, to an ocean's fulness,
>   Thy love and grace expand;
> Where glory, glory dwelleth,
>   In Emmanuel's land!

Let us try to grasp it: the quintessence of heaven's pure bliss for us will be just this, that with sinless minds, and raptured hearts, and perfected powers, through evolving aeons we shall be adoringly exploring an exhaustless Christ in whom are 'hid "all the treasures of wisdom and knowledge", and who ever-unfold-ingly expresses to us "the loving-kindness" which lives in the infinite heart of God. This is surely what Paul has in view when he writes, "That in the ages to come He might show the *exceeding* riches of His grace in His kindness toward us through Christ Jesus" (Eph. ii. 7). We read again and again in the New Testament about "grace" and even "riches of grace"; but there is only one place where this superlative occurs—"the *exceeding* riches of His grace", and it refers to "the *ages to come*".

In the lovely evolution of those "ages to come" there can be nothing static or stagnant. This wonderful Christ is bigger far than all our powers of imagination, while evermore He remains the "meek and lowly" One, our personal, sympathetic Companion, the All-in-all of each individual disciple. Even as Paul's concept of Christ grew and grew down here on earth, it was to go on developing in the Beyond. One of the most humbling discoveries which all men make who give themselves to hard study and much learning is that the more and more they know, so the more and more there is beyond them which they do *not* know. Each new knowing opens up some other vast stretch of *un*known. How many of us went to university or seminary proudly filled with all that we knew, and came out knowing most of all how *little* we knew! A little boy walked into the garden with his daddy late one evening. A big, bright, full-faced moon was just rising over the tree-tops. The little boy gave one delighted look at it, and then exclaimed, "Ooh, look! Get it, Daddy!" Many of us in supposed wisdom but unsuspected spiritual childhood have thought we could "get" Christ like that! We have taken Him as Saviour; we have read our daily "portion" in the Bible; we have "said our prayers" at morn or bed-time; and we have thought that this was all there was in knowing Christ. Such an idea is as infantile as the little fellow's notion that he could get the moon!

We are to know Him more and more, here on earth; then on, through those "ages to come", which stretch beyond, "His servants shall serve Him; and they shall see His face; and His name shall be in their foreheads; and there shall be no night . . ." (Rev. xxii. 3). In that light where there is never a shadow, we shall "see Him as He is" (1 John iii. 3), and begin to know Him as only heaven can reveal Him, in ever-bigger, ever-lovelier contexts! "That I may know Him" . . . *Him* . . . HIM! What is all else in heaven if *He* is not there? This must be the focuspoint even of our desires toward heaven—"That I may know *HIM*", or even heaven will disappoint us. Heaven is both a place and a state of pure rapture; and all its rapture centres in *HIM*. "Now we see through a glass darkly; but then face to face" (1 Cor. xiii. 12). Now it is from grace to grace; but then it will be "from glory to glory" (2 Cor. iii. 18). And *HE* will be both the spring and the ever-flowing continuity of it all.

CAN IT REALLY BE OURS?

For every pledge He ever spake
Is stamped by truth divine,
And I by trustful praying make
Each gracious promise mine.
He said that He would manifest
His presence with His own ;
And oft today in trystings blest
He makes His visits known.

J.S.B.

CAN IT REALLY BE OURS?

"That I may know Him . . ."—Phil. iii. 10.

Well, the question of moment is: May you and I know Christ in that increasingly absorbent way in which Paul learned to know Him, with similarly expanding mental apprehension and spiritual appropriation? I am sure the answer is, Yes. We wrong Paul as well as ourselves if we regard him as a privileged object of arbitrary divine favouritism. From the moment of his conversion he became singularly self-abasing, teachable, willing for self-sacrifice, determined to know Christ by study of God's Word, by protracted prayer, by witnessing and serving, by trusting and proving, and by counting all other things as less than nothing compared with "the excellency of the knowledge of Christ Jesus my Lord" (Phil. iii. 8). The Holy Spirit really had scope in Paul. Does He in you and me? One of our Lord's parting words was, "He that loveth Me shall be loved of My Father; and I will love Him, and will *manifest* Myself to him" (John xiv. 21). He is speaking of *spiritual* manifestations to the loving-hearted, prayerful-minded among His people. He is engaging Himself to you and me, if we believe Him and act upon it.

We were speaking earlier about the *need* for spiritual illumination by the Holy Spirit in our knowing of Christ. Let us now emphasise that we may truly *have* it, if we will give the Holy Spirit scope, as Paul did.

There is a notable paragraph about this spiritually-illumined "knowing" in Ephesians i. 15–23. It is a recorded prayer which begins: "That the God of our Lord Jesus Christ, the Father of glory, may give unto you the Spirit of wisdom (or insight) and of revelation (or unveiling) in the knowledge of Himself; the eyes of your understanding *being enlightened,* that ye may *know.* . . ."

Notice how Paul here prays for the Father to "*give*" the Holy Spirit to those early Ephesian believers. But had they not *already* received Him? Does not Paul himself tell them that they were already "*sealed*" by the Holy Spirit (i. 13, 14)? And is not the same true of *all* who are really Christ's? How then can Paul pray that God may "*give*" the Spirit to the already regenerate? It is because, as the Spirit of "*insight*" and of "*unveiling*", He is to be received ever-progressively. Even the Spirit-born and Spirit-sealed need supernatural illumination. It is a wonderful blessing to have good eyes; but what use are the best eyes without light in which to see? The Holy Spirit gave us new eyes at our regeneration, but our new sight needs new *light*; and even in the light we can only see what is revealed. Thus, even the saved and sealed need the "Spirit of insight and of unveiling", and may be illumined by Him *more and more*. There is an absolute finality about the work of Christ *for* us on the Cross; but there is *no* finality about this illuminating ministry of the Holy Spirit *in* us.

In his autobiography, the late Dr. R. W. Dale of Birmingham tells of an occasion when the Holy Spirit brought the truth of Christ's resurrection to his mind with overwhelming force. He was preparing an Easter sermon; and when about halfway through his preparation the truth of the resurrection suddenly broke in upon him with such stunning and yet thrilling effect that it affected all his ministry afterwards. Here are his own words—" 'Christ is alive,' I said to myself; 'alive!' And then I paused—'alive!' And then I paused again—'alive!' 'Can that really be true? Living as I myself am?' I got up and walked about repeating, 'Christ is living! Christ is living!' At first it seemed strange and hardly true; but at last it came upon me as a burst of sudden glory: yes, Christ is living! It was to me a new discovery. I thought that all along I had believed it; but not until that moment did I feel sure about it."

Those last words are arresting—"I thought that all along I had believed it; but not until that moment did I feel sure about it." We never really "*know*" spiritual truths—that is, in the vital, vivid, spiritual sense, until they are applied to the mind and heart under this illuminating power of the Holy Spirit. Did not our Lord say of the Holy Spirit, "He shall receive of Mine *and shall show it unto you*" (John xvi. 14)? When once we have come to "know" spiritual truths in this way we can never doubt them again; and not all the sophistries of human philosophy can ever deceive us into disbelieving them. We have come to "know" them in that inmost and deepmost part of our being which is even more fundamental in our human nature than our faculty of reason or intellect.

A certain young man used to come to our church, and listen appreciatively to the preaching of the Gospel. I was quite accustomed to seeing him there, for he always sat somewhere about the same place in the gallery. He seemed a quiet, thoughtful, respectable young fellow; but I could not be just sure whether he had entered into a saving experience of Christ or not. Then, one Sunday evening, while I was preaching, I noticed a different look come over him. It seemed to come quite suddenly. His attention became concentrated in a way I had never seen before. There was an almost strained look of earnestness. I noticed the same intensity the following week, and again the week after that. In fact, after the change on that first Sunday evening, his whole manner was different. He gave one the impression that he had come into the light of some great discovery. And so, indeed, he had; for he later told me so. He came to my vestry one Sunday evening, after the service, and told me how, from one electrifying moment in that recent evening service, he had seen spiritual truths with a vividness such as he had never known before, and had never dreamed possible. He had always more or less appreciated the Gospel truths which I had preached before then; but now— well, he simply could not put into words the change that had come over him. He somehow *saw* these truths now, as he had never done before. He *felt the power* of them, and grasped the terrific meaning of them, and was himself in the grip of them. Oh, why was it, he wanted to know, that other people did not see these things in the same way? What could be done to get these truths home to their hearts? He could be at ease about this no longer. He must do something, and had come to ask if I could offer him any guidance.

That young man illustrates what we have been saying. Even allowing for differences of temperament and circumstance, there is always something of that kind comes about when our minds and hearts are under this illuminating power of the Holy Spirit. Oh, that it were more commonly experienced among those of us who profess to be the Lord's!

It is noticeable that when Paul prays for the "Spirit of wisdom and revelation" to be given, it is "that ye may *know* . . ." Actually the Greek verb might be more exactly represented by our word *"see"*. Paul would have us *see* spiritual truths, as he himself did, with that inward luminousness which only the Holy Spirit can give them. And, oh, this vivifying ministry of the Spirit is real to the sanctified, prayerful mind! It has been well said that such a believer on his knees can see far more than the philosopher on his tip-toes!

By What Process?

But finally, to come right down to the plainly practical: *How* may you and I learn to know Christ in this direct and developing way? The answer, I believe, is threefold.

First we must more and more familiarise ourselves with Him *photographically* in the four Gospels. We may well be wary against having any mental image of Him deriving from supposed likenesses such as hang inside church premises or in Christian homes. No genuine portraiture of His human face has been handed down. All that artists can do is to picture Him as they *think* He must have been. It is wise to recall again the words of 2 Corinthians v. 16, "Yea, though we have known Christ after the flesh, yet now henceforth know we Him (thus) no more." Our Lord has His own way of "manifesting" Himself to the prayerful heart. I will not shrink from saying that the Christ who is inwardly luminous to my own mind, especially in times of prayer, is unlike any artist's picture of Him which I have ever seen, ancient or modern. Nor could I put on canvas that dear and shining Christ of my inward seeing, even if I were the cleverest artist who ever lived. And in speaking thus, I am only articulating what many others would say.

For one thing, we should ever remember that there is now an opalescent glory-light eradiating from His face and form which was not there during "the days of His flesh" here on earth (except once, on the Mount of Transfiguration); therefore no artist's picture or sculpture can possibly represent Him as He *now* is. Nor should we be over-anxious to receive *visions* of Him as we commune with Him or contemplate Him. There is a realising of His presence, and a seeing of His face, and a vivid joy of communion, which are quite independent of visions.

Years ago I used secretly to envy those persons of the type who have periodically recurring visions. I used to think that their spirituality must be superior to my own, or that perhaps they were special favourites of the Holy Spirit. Well, any such envy has gone. Too many of those so-called "visions" are neither normal nor healthful. I do not doubt either the possibility or the reality of such supernatural breakings-in upon human minds. I have known some which were undoubtedly genuine, though I myself have never had such experiences. Yet I am none the less convinced that many visions are simply the fond delusions of imaginative auto-suggestion.

But, quite independently of mental images, portraitures, and visionary beholdings, there is one place where we may "see Jesus" in just the very way that the Holy Spirit designs for *all* of us. It is in the four Gospels. There, in the inspired pen-photography of the Holy Spirit, through Matthew, Mark, Luke, and John, we see the real Jesus Christ living and moving before us. There we see Jesus as He really *was*, and as He still really *is*, in heart and mind and feeling and gracious disposition.

Oh, Christian believer, longing to know Christ as Paul knew Him, be persuaded of this: you and I need before all else to know the Lord Jesus of those four Gospel memoirs. As we read them (let us repeat it again for emphasis) we are learning to "know Him", not only as He was, but as He characteristically *abides*. All those same lines of meekness and majesty, lowliness and loftiness, exquisite nobility and tenderness, flaming severity against hypocrisy and indulgent selfishness, love of boys and girls, kindliness to the aged, sympathy with the poor and needy, and utter compassion to the contrite—all these are *still* Jesus, the Jesus whom we contact when we pray. No image or concept of Him is to be entertained which does not accord with what we have in those four Gospels. However prayerful or contemplative we may be, the moment our thinking of Jesus gets away from that New Testament standard we are in peril; we are devout but deceived; we are out of touch with the real Christ whom Paul knew; and our praying has vaporised into sentimental mysticism.

So, then, as a first counsel, I would earnestly advise an increasing *familiarity* with the four Gospels. We never finally know them, even when we think we do. They are always springing fresh surprises on us. Read them again and again and again. There is something new at every new reading. Linger over them.

Learn them. Traverse them so often that even without any effort to memorise them you find them taking permanent hold on mind and memory. It is wonderful how powerfully they come flooding back upon us in our times of praying, bringing Christ lucidly to the mind in vivid settings and characteristic attitudes such as are most suitable to our varying moods and thoughts in times of prayer-communion.

But besides this, we should keep reading, reading, reading in those four Gospels with a certain thought always dominating us. That is, we should be continually whispering to ourselves: "This Lord Jesus whom I am watching and hearing and learning to know in these Gospels, is the very One with whom I am directly in touch every time I withdraw for secret prayer." When such a thought controls a prayerful reader, the Gospels "come alive" in a new way.

I shall never forget the sudden new spell which the Gospels cast over my own mind when I started reading them again, inwardly saying to myself all the while: "In watching and hearing this Jesus who moves and speaks in these Gospels, I am watching and hearing none other than *the God who made the universe.*" Oh, how those immortal pages lived and thrilled with magnetic new splendour! I could not leave them alone, nor would *they* leave *me* alone! The very heart of the Eternal was being laid bare before me! As I saw the little boys and girls running to Jesus, and climbing on to His lap; as I marked His welcoming words, accompanied as they must have been by an eager smile and a strong caress, I was watching *God*, and learning how *He* feels towards boys and girls! As I saw Jesus appealed to by the loathsome leper; as I beheld Him, not only sympathising, but inwardly pained or *"moved* with *compassion"*, even "touching" as well as healing him, I keenly sensed as never before how the heart of *God* suffers with the suffering members of our fallen race. Through every paragraph the words of Jesus kept echoing within me, "He that hath seen Me hath seen the Father." Everywhere I was observing and learning what *God* is like, how *God* behaves, and how *God* reacts to human need. Even so, to go through the Gospels, over and over again, with the thought in mind: This is the very Lord Jesus with whom I am directly communing today, can have, and always *does* have, a deep influence upon us in our daily prayer-trysts.

But now, my second word of counsel is: Learn to know Christ *doctrinally* in the New Testament epistles. In the Gospels He is *presented* to us. In the epistles He is *interpreted* to us. Just as in the Gospels we learn who Jesus *was* (and *is*); what He said and did; how He felt and reacted; so in the epistles we learn all that He is "made unto *us*" (1 Cor. i. 30) as Christian believers, even "wisdom, righteousness, sanctification, and redemption". It is wonderful how those precious letters open up to us all the tender relationships which our dear Lord sustains to us as the people of His special treasure, and all the covenant provisions which are ours in Him. I am thinking cautiously and speaking deliberately when I say that in my own judgment there cannot be a deep, rich knowing of Christ apart from an intelligent familiarity with the New Testament epistles.

Think, for instance, what it means, in our prayer seasons, to have a mind steeped in the teachings of the Hebrews epistle concerning the heavenly priesthood of our Lord. Think what it means, in enlightened outreachings toward Christ, when prayer is winged heavenwards on the teachings of Ephesians concerning the threefold mystic union of our Lord and His people—Head and body; Bridegroom and bride; Foundation and building; a *living*, and a *loving*, and a *lasting* union!

To retire for secret prayer with a mind continually tutored in these priceless truths does more to open the floodgates of the soul, and to make our living Lord real, than words could easily convey. Some of us can give testimony to this from our own diary. "We speak that we do know, and testify that which we have seen" (John iii. 11). Nor is there any exercise in prayer more uplifting or sanctifying than to "talk over" with our listening Lord the high challenges and deep doctrines of the epistles, with a view to their fulfilment in our daily experience.

Our third and final counsel is: At all costs make time for regular, unhurried *daily engagement in prayer*. Nothing can take the place of this. There can be no direct and developing communion with Christ apart from it. We must meet Him often, and *linger* in His presence. Erratic irregularity, hurried snatches, and excited emergency-prayers, give our patient Master little opportunity of making Himself known to us; but if we really "hunger and thirst" after Him; if we rescue our prayer-times from the tyranny of our changing moods; if with steady tenacity we persevere in asking and seeking and knocking; it will not be too long before we find ourselves breaking out into such songs as,

> Lord, Thou hast made Thyself to me
> A living, bright reality.
> More present to faith's vision keen
> Than any outward object seen ;
> More dear, more intimately nigh
> Than e'en the closest earthly tie.

In any case, we ought to pray regularly as a Christian *duty*; yet the sooner our prayer-times are lifted from the level of "duty" to that of *delight*, the better.

Likely enough, for some time, we may find our longer praying apparently unrewarding, perhaps even discouraging. We must guard against hasty and pessimistic conclusions. The fault lies, not in prayer, but in our own selves. We are far more earthy, far more obtuse, far more unyielded than we suspect. We must keep on. The preliminary testings of faith and patience are a refining, spiritualising discipline. If we will only keep on, believing in His real presence and loving faithfulness, this is what will eventually happen: there will come a moment, a quiet but strangely thrilling moment, when quite suddenly though silently we shall know with inward certainty and rapture that we are really *through* to God!—that all heaven is *open* above us!—that prayer is *real!*—that we are really at the feet of our manifested Lord!

From that moment prayer will never be hard in the same way any more; and life itself can never be the same again. A few experiences of that kind, and prayer will become, as it was with Paul, the most natural and exhilarating activity of the mind. Spiritual things will become the *real* things. Christ will be the excellent treasure compared with which all earthly things are mere dross. Some of our friends may not understand us, and there may be other penalties to the flesh; but Christ will have become a very heaven of joy to us, and all earthly deprivations will have become more than compensated for by the superabounding consolations of His love. That, however, is only the sunrise! That is only the beginning! It is then that our hearts will begin really to blend with Paul's in crying out, *"That I may know Him . . . !"*

THE POWER OF HIS RESURRECTION

"Oh, live in me this day,
Oh, clothe Thyself, Thy purpose, yet again
    in human clay.
Work through my feebleness Thy strength.
Work through my meanness Thy nobility.
Work through my helpless poverty of soul
    Thy grace, Thy glory, and Thy love."

Anon.

THE POWER OF HIS RESURRECTION

"That I may know Him, and the power of His resurrection."—Phil. iii. 10.

WHAT infinitudes in one short phrase—"the power of His resurrection"! What vistas the super-victory of that vacated sepulchre opens up! "Our Saviour Jesus Christ hath abolished death, and hath brought life and immortality to light through the Gospel" (2 Tim. i. 10)! You and I are meant now to know "the power of His resurrection" toward ourselves as Christian believers.

How vital is its *evidential* power! The classic Corinthian passage on the subject makes it the prime apologetic of the Christian religion: "If Christ be not raised, your faith is vain" (1 Cor. xv. 17).

How complete is its *justifying* power! He was "delivered up for our offences, and was raised again for our justification" (Rom. iv. 25). "Who shall lay anything to the charge of God's elect? It is God that justifieth. Who is he that condemneth? Christ died, yea rather, is risen again . . ." (Rom. viii. 33, 34).

How wonderful is its *quickening* power! We are "raised up together" with Him in spiritual union. We "walk in newness of life", and "sit together" with Him "in the heavenlies" (Rom. vi. 4, Eph. ii. 6).

How reassuring is its *certifying* power! What greater public proof could there be that the atonement is accepted?—that Satan is defeated?—that the power of death is broken? (Rom. v. 10, 2 Tim. ii. 14). "God hath given assurance unto all men in that He hath raised Him from the dead" (Acts xvii. 31).

How unmistakable is its *demonstrative* power!—especially in relation to our Lord Jesus. "Destroy this temple," He says, "and in three days I will raise it up" (John ii. 19–21). He said it; and He did it. "I lay down my life. . . . I have power to lay

it down, and I have power to take it again" (John x. 17, 18).
He is "declared to be the Son of God with power . . . by the
resurrection from the dead" (Rom. i. 4).

How precious is its *consolatory* power! The risen Victor is the
tenderhearted Saviour who not only "ever liveth to make intercession" for us, but is "touched with the feeling of our infirmities", and is our constant Companion "all the days, even unto
the end of the age" (Heb. vii. 25, iv. 15, Matt. xxviii. 20).

How titanic, in prospect, is its *re-animating* power! "Now is
Christ risen from the dead, and become the firstfruits of them
that are fallen asleep" (1 Cor. xv. 20). That is, He is the pledge
and specimen of the mighty harvest yet to be. The graves shall
be emptied. In their millions the departed shall reappear, re-
clothed in bodily form. "As in Adam all die, so in Christ shall all
be made alive" (1 Cor. xv. 22).

Amid a world blinded by Satan and blighted by sin and blasted
by war, amid the crash of armies and the crash of wrecked hopes,
amid the pathetic breakdown of human nature and the ironic
failure of proud, little twentieth-century man to work out his own
salvation—amid all this, and amid the gloomy problems which
beset the immediate future, the one great fact which gives solid
comfort and hope and promise is the fact that nineteen hundred
and some years ago, on the sixteenth day of the month Nisan,
A.D. 32, God raised up the crucified Jesus Christ from the grave.
That empty tomb means Diabolos vanquished and Christ victorious. It means that in the next chapter of human history God's
kingdom will come, and His will be done on earth as it is done
in heaven. The biggest of problems to the natural man in this
present age is the silence of God. "Why does not God speak?"
he asks. "Let God speak, so that we may hear Him and know
that He really *is*." The resurrection of Christ proclaims that God
has spoken already, and that the God who spoke yesterday will
speak again in a soon-coming tomorrow. As truly as He rose,
Christ will come again. His resurrection tolls the knell on evil's
dark kingdom, and rings the glad bell of God-given hope for the
travailing earth. The present age (we verily believe) is rushing
on, with accentuated momentum, to the world's Friday night; the
morning of the Millennial seventh-day thousand-year Sabbath is
soon to break, when the Christ of the Easter morn shall become

the Christ of the Davidic throne; when swords shall become ploughshares, and spears become pruning-hooks, and the nations shall learn war no more.

Such is the significance of our Lord's resurrection for human history; and it is well that we should gratefully keep it in mind during days like these. But besides this, let all of us who know the cleansing efficacy of our Saviour's precious blood, and the regenerating reality of the Holy Spirit, pray that the "Spirit of wisdom and of revelation" may vivify it all afresh to us, causing it to thrill us, and grip us, and impel us onward in the train of our Lord's triumph.

This brings me to observe that when Paul expressed his ever-insistent urge—"That I may know Him, and the power of His resurrection", he was thinking not so much of its evidential power, or its justifying power, or its quickening power, or its certifying power, or its demonstrative power, or its consolatory power, or its re-animative power. All those were exuberantly taken for granted between him and his beloved Philippians. What he now wanted increasingly to prove was its *liberating* power in mind and heart and life. He wanted to know more of its emancipating and transforming power in daily experience, in the overcoming of evil, and in witnessing for Christ. And it is *that* aspect of it which specially concerns us in this present study.

As a preliminary, reflect for a moment how "the power of His resurrection" is exhibited in our Lord Jesus Himself. First, it publicly crowns His victory over *self*. Right from that first open encounter with Satan when the tempter said, "Command that these stones be made bread", and our Lord replied, "Man shall not live by bread alone", He had answered a firm "No" to every movement of His human nature which would in any way have infringed upon His utter loyalty to the Father's will; until, in the Garden of Gethsemane, He became "obedient unto death, even the death of the Cross" (Phil. ii. 8). And now, that emptied sepulchre culminatively acknowledges His complete victory over the human self.

Second, His resurrection proclaims His victory over *sin*. "By one man sin entered into the world, and death by sin; and so death passed upon all men, for all have sinned" (Rom. v. 12). By raising and exalting Christ, the Father now gives crowning attestation that there is *no* sin in His incarnate Son. Had there been sin in Him, death could have held His body along with all others; but where there is no sin death has no hold. Therefore, as Peter says, in Acts ii. 24, "It was *not possible* (i.e. not with moral consistency) that *He* should be holden of it."

Next, His resurrection manifests His victory over *death*. In the Scriptures there are nine instances of other persons who were brought back to life; but all those persons died again. Theirs was merely a temporary resuscitation, not real resurrection. In sheer contrast, our Lord rose and now "liveth in the power of an endless life" (Heb. vii. 16). "In that He died, He died unto sin once for all; but in that He liveth, He liveth unto God." "Death hath no more dominion over Him" (Rom. vi. 9, 10). Our Lord has an *immortal* human body, a human body which disease can never infect and death can never destroy. In Himself actually, and for His people potentially, He has for evermore overcome the power of death and hades.

And, once more, His resurrection openly signalises His victory over *Satan,* the leader and instigator of the insurrectionist movement in God's universe. At last, One stronger than the strong has come to the rescue, and has broken the power of sin in human nature. The guileless soul of Jesus sees right through the subtlest wiles of the tempter, and snaps their ensnaring spell. All that the foiled and fuming arch-fiend can do with that stainless Standard-bearer of divine truth is to perpetrate through wicked accomplices on earth His gross abuse and shameful death on the Cross. But in so doing, the gloating Apollyon oversteps himself. The deceiver is deceived. The defeater is defeated. The unretaliating Victim becomes the divinely vindicated Victor, for He transforms that Cross into His supreme act of voluntary self-surrender to the overruling will of God, thereby breaking the hitherto unbroken power of Satan over human nature. His resurrection inflicts a staggering reverse on the humiliated enemy before the watching eyes of a myriad spirit-intelligences in the invisible realm who now behold with wonder the mighty power of God "which He wrought in Christ when He raised Him from the dead, and set Him at His own right hand in the heavenlies, far above every principality and might and dominion, and every name that is named. . . ."—including all the rebel "principalities and powers" under Satan's leadership (Eph. i. 20, 21, iii. 10).

Yes, mark it well: Paul does not stop even when he has said that Christ is actually at the right hand of God. He must needs add, "Far above all principality and power and might and dominion, and every name that is named, not only in this age, but also in that which is to come". The great apostle is referring to those evil spirit-beings who are confederate with Satan in his wicked designs against God and the souls of men. They are referred to again in Ephesians iii. 10, where Paul tells us that the "manifold wisdom of God" has now been displayed to these "principalities and powers in the heavenly spheres" through the *Church*, which was God's hidden secret during preceding centuries. And again we read of them in chapter vi. 12, where Paul writes, "For we wrestle not against flesh and blood, but against principalities, against powers, against the world-rulers of the darkness of this age, against the spirit-hosts of wickedness in the heavenly spheres".

No doubt when Paul wrote the words, "Far above *all* principality and power and might and *every* name that is named", he was referring comprehensively to *all* the various ranks and strata of living intelligences in the spirit world, unfallen as well as fallen, for Christ is over them all; but it is plain that the special reference is to those evil seditionists who war against holiness under the traitorous generalship of Satan. Were those powers and their dark-minded leader quiescent when God raised up Jesus from the dead and set Him at His own right hand? Are we not to understand that they would exert all their combined influence to obstruct it?

Even when our incarnate Lord was but a babe, did not Satan seek to slay Him by the sword of wicked Herod? Did not the arch-rebel endeavour with deceptive craftiness to seduce Him at the very outset of His public ministry? Was it not Beelzebub who incited the townsmen of Jesus to hurl Him over the precipice at Nazareth? Was it not the same evil one who lurked behind all the other plottings to kill Him, until at last he found an open door into the avaricious mind of Judas, and thus brought about our Lord's crucifixion? Can we think, then, that Satan was willing for our Lord's spirit to come back out of Hades, and for His body to arise out of its sepulchre on that first Easter morning? Do we not recall that until that hour Satan had "held the power of death" (Heb. ii. 14)? Has not Satan shown himself very jealous about dead bodies? Are we not told, in Jude 9, that Satan "disputed about the body of Moses"? Maybe if Satan had managed to get his way Moses would never have appeared in that body of his on the Mount of Transfiguration. We do not know about that for certain, but we do know this, that Satan maliciously injected sin and death into our race, that he has tyrannically wielded "the power of death", and that least of all did he want the sinless Jesus to elude him.

But there is more even than that. It would seem that Satan was once the rightful "prince of this world". Our Lord called him by that title, though in its now-evil sense. Moreover, when Satan boasted the power to give our Lord Jesus "all the kingdoms of the world", our Lord did not contradict it. Satan knew well enough that our Lord was the incarnate Son of God, the new representative Man. He knew also that his own power had been broken in the human race by our Lord's sinless, utter obedience to God the Father. Yes, Satan knew that; and he also knew that for Jesus to rise from the dead in the union of a sinless soul and a deathless body must mean salvation for men, and the end of his own evil usurpation.

Yet see now what happened. At last there was One who had broken the power of sin and Satan in human nature, and who therefore need *not* die (for since He was sinless death had no claim). But that solitary One who need *not* die, voluntarily *did* die for the sake of others. Hades had absolutely no power over His sinless spirit, and the grave had absolutely no claim to that undefiled body. As Peter said on the day of Pentecost, "It was *impossible* that He should be holden of it". Irresistibly He rose from Hades and the grave, wresting the very "*keys* of Hades and death" from the devil's grasp (Rev. i. 18). Then, in that sinless, resurrected, all-victorious manhood, He ascended up "above all the heavens" (Eph. iv. 10) and against all the fuming opposition of Satanic adversaries, to the very throne of God, in triumphant subjugation of all the powers and spheres! Man, whom Satan dragged from his throne in Eden, now reigns as the *new* Man on the very throne of heaven!

Such, then, is "the power of His resurrection" as exhibited in our Lord Jesus Himself. But there is something further, something even bigger involved in it, which potently relates it all to the millions of Christ's people. He has risen as *our Representa-*

tive, with all would-be intruders beneath His feet, and with administrative authority to make all this "power of His resurrection" operative toward His redeemed ones. Through the effusion of the Holy Spirit upon the whole Church at Pentecost, and the continuing *infusion* of that same Holy Spirit among His people individually, our Lord comes back to us invisibly, omnipresently, to share the "spoils of victory" with us (Isa. liii. 12); so that "the power of His resurrection" thereby becomes experientially communicable to each of us—spiritually here and now; physically at the age-end translation; then unendingly through "the ages to come"! What we are now to investigate somewhat is how *you and I* may know "the power of His resurrection" in our own day-by-day experience as Christian believers.

Be reminded, just here, that Paul's phrase, "the power of His resurrection", occurs in the third chapter of Philippians. In that context, beginning at verse 10, Paul evidently has this matter of resurrection-life much in mind, and in the closing sentences of the chapter he shows how the believer's resurrection-life is to be culminated at the second coming of Christ. Read verses 20 and 21 again:

"For our citizenship is in heaven, from whence also we look for the Saviour, the Lord Jesus Christ; who shall change our body of humiliation, that it may be fashioned like unto His body of glory, according to the working whereby He is able to subdue all things to Himself."

The resurrection-power of our Lord always operates in the three ways indicated in those verses. First, it is a *subduing* power— "according to the working whereby He is able even to subdue all things to Himself". That subduing power will have a climactic demonstration in the coming translation of the saints; but there is also an advance operation of it here and now, in the subduing of evil tempers, unruly tongues, flaming passions, enslaving desires, inordinate ambitions, fear, pride, hate, jealousy, temptation, circumstance, and innate proclivities to sin. It is grandly real to those who are living in it. A crowned Christ in a consecrated heart means real victory over self and sin and Satan, through the continuous operation of "the power of His resurrection".

Second, "the power of His resurrection" is a *transforming* power within us. Glance again at that last verse of the chapter. By His resurrection-power our Lord is going to "transform this body of our humiliation, that it may be fashioned like unto the body of His glory". There is an anticipative fulfilment also of *that* in those yielded hearts where He reigns as King. By "the power of His resurrection" He transforms the character, conforming it more and more to His own.

Third, "the power of His resurrection" is a *vitalising* power already operating in us in a way which anticipates its ultimate expression at our Lord's return. All of our ministering, our speaking and writing, our serving and organising, our witness for Christ both in public and in private, has an inward glow and a communicative vitality which gives it *telling-power*—far more at times than we ourselves sense, as the resurrection-life fills us.

There may still be opposition, for there will always be those who resist Spirit-given *witness* even though they cannot refute Spirit-given *wisdom*. Those Jewish leaders of the first century could not answer the wisdom either of our Lord or of Stephen, yet they slew them both. We must never aggravate opposition; nor must we be surprised when it comes. Overcoming wisdom and spiritual power will be given at each emergency. Often we shall be mightiest when we seem weakest. Whenever a Stephen is martyred, there is always a Saul—a future apostle Paul—looking on, and about to be converted! We find, as Paul found, that when we are weakest (in ourselves) we are strongest (in Christ), and we learn to say with him, "I will rather glory in my infirmities, that *the power of Christ* may rest upon me!"

> Yes, He's the One who now is my dear Saviour;
> A Saviour living *in* me, hour by hour!
> Now every day He keeps me brave and tranquil,
> And conquers sin within me by His power.
> He lives within, my heavenly Friend and Keeper.
> He breaks the cords by which I have been bound.
> I love to tell His name—His name is *JESUS*.
> Yes, He's the risen, living Saviour I have found!

RESURRECTION LIFE TYPIFIED

"That I may know Him." Ah, I long to know
Not just a Christ of far-gone years ago ;
Nor even reigning on a heavenly throne,
Too high and distant to be really known.
I long to know him closely ; this is how,
Alive—and in this ever-pressing "now" ;
Communicating His all-conquering power,
A living One, within my heart this hour,
Who now no longer lives from me apart,
But shares His resurrection in my heart.

J.S.B.

RESURRECTION LIFE TYPIFIED

". . . and the power of His resurrection"—Phil. iii. 10.

THOSE who take a "modernist" view of the Bible, whether that of the now out-moded "Higher Critics" or that of the Barthian and Brunnerian "Neo-Orthodoxy", will have a "blind spot" toward the latent typology of the Old Testament. We on our part can only marvel that they are so blind to it. Of this we are sure, that when the so-called "Neo-Orthodoxy" has drooped exhausted to its grave, the imperishable apologetic and endless surprise of this typological content will still be causing the Old Testament to "come alive" with new relevances and anticipations.

As we have said, elsewhere, the best illustrations of New Testament doctrine are those which we find in Old Testament story. Nor is that surprising, for the Bible is one interwoven whole. The New Testament is *en*folded in the Old, and the Old is *un*folded in the New. Every major doctrine of the New Testament is matched by some illuminating type or illustration in the Old.

Now there is in the Old Testament a most arresting pictorial anticipation of what it means to live and serve in the power of Christ's resurrection. Indeed, I think we may safely regard it as a Spirit-designed *type,* for the correspondences are too remarkable to be merely accidental. The spiritual value of such types is that they give to doctrine a graphic depiction which it could never have when simply stated in so many words. They make the truth live and move, and glow and grow, and linger there before our mental vision. They objectify doctrine for us, as on a television screen, making it vivid and captivating, filling out the meaning for us, and making it more easily grasped by our minds. Moreover, we go back to such types again and again, repeatedly discovering in them new turns and slants, new latencies and relevancies, so that they are a continual vein of wealth.

Perhaps it may not come as a surprise when we say that the special Old Testament type of living in "the power of His resurrection" is the prophet *Elisha*. Take another careful look at him, and see how this is so.

Remember first that except for our Lord Jesus, the prophet Elisha was the greatest *miracle-worker* who ever lived. He wrought far more miracles than his fiery predecessor, Elijah; and even more than the venerable lawgiver, Moses. Probably he performed others, too, besides those which are recorded in Scripture, for in 2 Kings viii. 4 we find King Jehoram asking Gehazi, "Tell me, I pray thee, all the great things that Elisha hath done." Elisha was distinctively the miracle-worker.

Observe, also, that running through Elisha's miracles there is a predominating characteristic. It is the operation of a life-power or *resurrection-energy* overcoming the blight and down-drag of death. Think back over Elisha's miracles. The first, after his return from Elijah's translation, is the healing of the death-spreading waters around Jericho. Instead of healthy crops and fruits and harvests there was always sterility and barrenness because the waters were brackish and deadly. Elisha now says: "Thus saith Jehovah, I have healed these waters; there shall not be from thence any more death or barren land" (2 Kings ii. 19–22). Henceforth death is overcome by life, instead of life by death.

The second miracle is the providing of water for the armies of Judah and Israel as they are threatened by death from drought in the desert (iii. 19–22). The third is the saving of the widow's sons and their distraught mother from servitude and death, by that wonderful cruse of oil which keeps pouring out supply until the rescue-money is provided (iv. 1–7). Next comes the mighty exploit of raising the Shunamite's dead son to life (iv. 18–37). Next comes the healing of the noxious pottage. As the sons of the prophets are eating they suddenly sense danger, and cry out, "There is death in the pot!" But Elisha transforms "death in the pot" to healthful food (iv. 38–41). On the heels of this comes the miraculous multiplication of the barley loaves among the dearth-plagued people (iv. 42–44). Then comes the cleansing of Naaman from his deadly leprosy, by the sevenfold ablution in Jordan (v. 1–19). And next, to mention just one more, we have the miracle of the restored axe-head. One of the sons of the prophets is felling wood near the river brink when the axe-head flies from the haft and falls into the water. "Alas!" exclaims the unhappy brother, "for it was borrowed." That is usually the kind of thing that happens when we borrow! Elisha, however, stands where the axe-head has fallen in, and by that wonderful resurrection-energy which all the while operates through him he recalls the iron so that it floats on the surface, overcoming the down-pull of gravitation, and causing the amazed spectators to exclaim, "The iron doth swim!"

Well, there it is; this death-conquering energy is seen in a peculiarly unmistakable way operating through the ministry of this man, making him a type to us who are the people of Christ, and objectifying what it means for *us*, in a spiritual sense, to live in "the power of His resurrection".

Does someone think we are fancifully "reading into" the narratives what is not really there? Then let me mention that our seeing this significance in Elisha receives a kind of addendum endorsement a bit further on, in 2 Kings xiii. 20, 21. As many of us have found, the Bible has its own way of letting you know whether you are following a right line or not. If a theory or interpretation is right, incidental corroborations keep turning up. If a theory or interpretation is wrong, then at some point or another awkward verses begin to lie athwart it which can only be made to fit by wresting them. Fascination with a theory has often led well-meaning expositors to tamper with plain meanings; and this has given rise to the slur that you can "make the Bible teach anything you want". Well, as we began to say, there is in 2 Kings xiii. 20, 21, a post-mortem corroboration that we are right in seeing this resurrection-energy operating typically through Elisha. Perhaps there is scarcely a queerer little episode in the Old Testament. Here it is.

"And Elisha died, and they buried him. And bands of the Moabites invaded the land at the coming in of the year.

"And it came to pass as they (certain Israelites) were burying a man, that, behold, they spied a band of men (Moabites); and they cast the man into the sepulchre of Elisha. And when the man was let down, and touched the bones of Elisha, *he revived, and stood up on his feet.*"

So, even after Elisha's demise, this eerie final touch is added, to make sure that we perceive his typical significance!

Does someone *still* think we are fancifully "reading into" the narratives what is not really there? Then let me offer a reminder as to how all this miracle-ministry *began*. It began over across the Jordan. Elisha's great master, the prophet Elijah, crossed the Jordan; from where he ascended to heaven in a whirlwind chariot of fire; and as he ascended he let fall his mantle upon Elisha. The type-parallel is surely unmistakable. Just as Elisha's great master went through the Jordan, so *our* great Elijah, the Lord Jesus, went through the Jordan of His Calvary death. Just as Elisha's master, after crossing the Jordan, ascended visibly to heaven, so *our* glorious Master similarly ascended visibly to heaven. And just as Elisha's master, in ascending, sent down his prophetic mantle upon his follower; so *our* ascended Master sent down the Holy Spirit, *His* mantle of spiritual enduement, upon *His* followers here on earth.

Elisha, then, is a significant figure. He is even more so when viewed in relation to his times. He lived in a day of large and brazen apostasy from the Jehovah faith, in the period heading up in that fearful judgment-crash which finally disintegrated the ten-tribed northern kingdom of Israel. Before that fateful climax came, God sent three extraordinary prophets to appeal and to warn, namely, Elijah, Elisha, and Jonah. They each gave the most remarkable signs from Jehovah. Elijah did the hitherto unheard-of miracle: he raised the dead. So did Elisha, along with a succession of supernatural doings which must have made the ears of his countrymen tingle. Then, through Jonah, came the most astonishing sign of all. In a symbolic way he not only died, but went down into sheol or hades, and re-emerged in resurrection! Then, with his body bleached white (as I suppose) from his strange sojourn in the sea-monster, he went to Nineveh and preached the biggest city on earth to repentance. Of course, the queer story of that jettisoned Hebrew prophet had reached Nineveh from the lips of the seagoing traders before ever Jonah himself turned up there. He was immediately the strangest cynozure ever seen there. The leaders and people recognised in him a sign from the God of heaven. They heeded his message; and Nineveh (larger in size than modern London!) repented in sackcloth. So Nineveh was spared.

Yet Jonah's own countrymen, the covenant people, Israel, were so infatuatedly married to their idolatries and obscenities that they remained impervious to all those abnormal signs. Through those three prophets, Elijah, Elisha, Jonah, their covenant God was showing them how He could raise *them* from the dead, nationally, if *they* would repent and return to Him; but they would have none of it; until God could only say through the sobbing prophet, Hosea, "Ephraim is joined to idols: *let him alone*" (Hos. iv. 17). It is an awful thing when the sinner is so far gone in determined impenitence that God has to say, "Let him alone." That is what happened to the ten-tribed northern kingdom of Israel. In 721 B.C., judgment fell. Samaria was destroyed; and the incorrigible people were swept into the Assyrian captivity, from which they never returned.

Of course, those preachers of today who are too "modern" to accept the miraculous elements in the narrative will see no such latent significance in Elijah, Elisha, Jonah. How much they miss! And what an irony that they should still be called "Modernists" when they are now decades out of date (especially archæologically)! As for ourselves, not only do we gratefully discern "the latent behind the patent" in that prophet-trio, but we also sense a disturbing parallel between *their* times and *ours*. Just as Elisha lived in that period which was heading toward the supreme judgment-crash upon his people, so, unless many of us are strangely mistaken, *we* are living in the period heading up to the globe-circling climax of the present age. The splitting of the atom has catapulted us into that end-epoch which our Lord foretold when He said, "Except those days should be shortened, there should no flesh be saved; but for the elect's sake those days shall be shortened" (Matt. xxiv. 22).

Yes, Elisha's times parallel with our own. There is a super-crisis ahead. In one sense this gladdens us, and lifts up our heads, for "the coming of the Lord draweth nigh", and our translation is at hand. But it also accentuates our concern (or *should* do) for those around us who are unprepared, unbelieving, and in many cases light-heartedly indifferent. In these days God is looking for Elishas—consecrated Christian believers, men and women, younger and older, who are *living and witnessing for Christ in "the power of His resurrection"*.

Now I can well imagine that by this time someone is saying: "Please let all this be taken for granted. Come right to the point, and tell us how to *get into* this living in the power of His resurrection. We are only too disappointed with our present dull average, and are only too eager for a richer spiritual life. We are awake to the urgency of the hour, and long to be our Lord's Elishas; but somehow the secret eludes us. Show us the *way into* this experience, this living in 'the power of His resurrection' ".

Well, we shall let *Elisha* tell us; and he speaks very clearly. He says that the way in is threefold:

       1. We must be sincere Christian believers.
       2. We must exercise faith for the blessing.
       3. We must cross Jordan with our Master.

We learn these three things in three distinct pictures which we have of Elisha. Turn, first, to 1 Kings xix. 19–21. This is where young-man Elisha first comes on the scene; and this is what we read:

"So Elijah departed thence, and found Elisha the son of Shaphat, who was plowing with twelve yoke of oxen before him, and he with the twelfth: and Elijah passed by him, and cast his mantle upon him.

"And he left the oxen, and ran after Elijah and said, Let me, I pray thee, kiss my father and my mother, and then I will follow thee. And he said unto him, Go back again: for what have I done to thee?

"And he returned back from him, and took a yoke of oxen, and slew them, and boiled their flesh with the instruments of the oxen, and gave unto the people, and they did eat. Then he arose, and went after Elijah, and ministered unto him."

In this episode three things stand out, the first of which is Elijah's *casting of his mantle* upon Elisha. The young ploughman knew at once what it meant. That is why he replied, "Let me, I pray thee, kiss my father and my mother; and then *I will follow thee.*" That casting of the mantle was the understood call to discipleship and the prophetic office. I am glad that Elisha was a *busy* young man. God usually calls those who are willing workers. I am glad, too, that Elisha was *affectionate* toward his parents; that he must needs consult them, and seek their blessing, and kiss them goodbye. Obedience to God should increase, not diminish, our affection to kith and kin.

Elisha's response to that mantle signifies, in type, that he was what we should nowadays call a *converted man.* His public discipleship and following of Elijah meant that in the face of widespread, popular apostasy from the religion of Israel's Holy Scriptures, Elisha 'now openly avowed himself a believer in Jehovah as the one true God, and a witness for Him along with the protestant reform movement of Elijah.

Besides this, Elisha now became a *separated* believer. So far as the records inform us, he never went back to his old life. He made a clean and final break.

What is more, he became an *active* believer. His was no passive profession. "He arose, and went after Elijah, and *ministered* unto him."

Converted, separated, active; that is where you and I must *begin,* if we would learn what it means to live in the power of our Lord's resurrection. Even assuming that we are truly *converted* to Christ, and "born again" of the regenerating Spirit, are we living the *separated* life? Do we find our pleasures in the things of the world? Do we allow compromises and indulgences which grieve the Holy Spirit and impoverish our spiritual life? Do we boast in the name of Christian "liberty" that we can "go places", or do this and that and the other thing, while all the time, deep in our hearts, there is uneasiness?

There is a sacred territory which lies exclusively between each soul and God, into which no other has a right to intrude. We must therefore guard against censoriously judging our Christian brethren in things which honestly appear right to them but seem wrong to us. Yet after we respectfully allow for that, there remains a fairly clearly demarcated area which by general consensus of the spiritually minded is forbidden ground to those who would be well-pleasing to our Lord. Again and again the New Testament calls us to separation from "the world". "Know ye not that the friendship of the world is enmity with God? Whosoever therefore will be a friend of the world is the enemy of God" (Jas. iv. 4). "Love not the world, neither the things that are in the world. If any man love the world, the love of the Father is not in him" (1 John ii. 15). The Spirit's call undoubtedly is, "Wherefore come out from among them, and be ye separate, saith the Lord, and touch not the unclean thing; and I will receive you, and will be a Father unto you; and ye shall be my sons and daughters, saith the Lord Almighty" (2 Cor. vi. 17, 18).

Whether it be palatable or otherwise does not unduly concern us, but we will not conceal our own conviction, after long observation, that there is no living in "the power of His resurrection" without a godly, consistent separation from the pleasures of the world and the indulgence of the flesh. Alas, many are not willing to pay this price.

Then, besides separation, there must be *active* discipleship. How often do we intercede before God for the unsaved? How often do we take the name of Jesus on our lips in witness to them? When did we last give out a tract or book, or write a letter, with a view to someone's conversion? Are we linked up with a sound, Bible-teaching church? and are we continually seeking to bring souls under the preaching of the Word?

Converted, separated, active: yes, these are necessary prerequisites. Yet although all three were exemplified in the faithful Elisha, he was not yet into that big blessing which made him a type of living in the power of Christ's resurrection. The next step (and it did not come until about ten years after his conversion) was that he must *exercise faith for the blessing*. We learn this from the narrative leading up to Elijah's translation, in 2 Kings ii. 1–6.

(1) "And it came to pass, when the Lord would take up Elijah into heaven by a whirlwind, that Elijah went with Elisha from Gilgal.
(2) And Elijah said unto Elisha, Tarry here, I pray thee; for the Lord hath sent me to Beth-el. And Elisha said unto him, As the Lord liveth, and as thy soul liveth, I will not leave thee. So they went down to Beth-el.
(3) And the sons of the prophets that were at Beth-el came forth to Elisha, and said unto him, Knowest thou that the Lord will take away thy master from thy head today? And he said, Yea, I know it; hold ye your peace.
(4) And Elijah said unto him, Elisha, tarry here, I pray thee; for the Lord hath sent me to Jericho. And he said, As the Lord liveth, and as thy soul liveth, I will not leave thee. So they came to Jericho.
(5) And the sons of the prophets that were at Jericho came to Elisha, and said unto him, Knowest thou that the Lord will take away thy master from thy head today? And he answered, Yea, I know it; hold ye your peace.
(6) And Elijah said unto him, Tarry, I pray thee, here; for the Lord hath sent me to Jordan. And he said, As the Lord liveth, and as thy soul liveth, I will not leave thee. So they two went on."

We gather that Elijah must have informed Elisha about the impending translation. Elisha knew that he could not carry on Elijah's work without Elijah's power, and had evidently said so to his master. But Elijah must have replied (as we find echoed in verse 10) that so long as he himself remained here the power would not come upon Elisha, but that when he (Elijah) departed it would come (just as our Lord said to His disciples, "Nevertheless, I tell you the truth: it is expedient for *you* that *I* go away; for if I go not away the Paraclete will not come unto you; but if I depart I will send Him unto you").

From then onwards Elisha determined that he would never leave his great master until somehow the power was his. That is, he started exercising faith for the blessing. Yet alongside of that it seemed as though his master was trying to shake him off. See verse 2: "And Elijah said unto Elisha: Tarry here (Gilgal), I pray thee; for the Lord hath sent me to Beth-el." Now Bethel was one of the two main centres of the illicit cult of the golden calf (Dan in the north and Bethel in the south). Elisha was far from popular there! It was there, shortly after, that the young men (not "little children" as in Authorised Version) taunted him, "Go up, thou bald head. Go up, thou bald head", meaning, of course, "Go up in the air and vanish, just as Elijah did". However, when Elijah recommended Elisha to tarry at Gilgal, the determined disciple was not to be put off, for he replied, "As the Lord liveth, and as thy soul liveth, *I will not leave thee.*"

The same thing happened when they reached Bethel. "And Elijah said unto him: Elisha, tarry here, I pray thee; for the Lord hath sent me to Jericho. And he (Elisha) said: As the Lord liveth, and as thy soul liveth, *I will not leave thee.*"

And the same thing happened again at Jericho. "Elijah said unto him: Tarry, I pray thee, here; for the Lord hath sent me to Jordan." This must have made Elisha wonder indeed where the journey would *end*; yet he staunchly persisted, "As the Lord liveth, and as thy soul liveth, *I will not leave thee.*"

But besides these seeming discouragements from his master, there were discouragements from other believers. See verse 3: "And the sons of the prophets that were at Beth-el came forth to Elisha, and said unto him: Knowest thou that the Lord will take away thy master from thy head today? And he (Elisha) said: Yea, I know it; *hold ye your peace.*" See also verse 5: "And the sons of the prophets that were at Jericho came to Elisha, and said unto him: Knowest thou that the Lord will take away thy master from thy head today? And he (Elisha) answered: Yea, I know it; *hold ye your peace.*"

It just seemed as though both his master and those other believers were bent on discouraging Elisha; but he held on, without doubting his master, and without heeding other voices. And how it all speaks to Christian believers today! If, with a deep sense of need, we set our minds on some big blessing, our faith is always tested. Somehow, in the very nature of things at present, it cannot be otherwise. It may seem as though even the Lord Himself is trying to shake us off, and that those among the Lord's people who ought to help us most are our worst hinderers. How many seekers after holiness and the enduing of the Spirit have given up, either because they were not forewarned of such discouragements or were not able to endure them! We must learn to hang on to *our* Master as Elisha did to his; and we may have to say to other believers what Elisha said to the sons of the prophets—"Hold ye your peace!" There are always those who will say to us, "You are converted; you are saved; you are going to heaven; you are living a good life; why need you become an oddity or an extremist?"

But now comes the third thing, the decisive crisis-point in the story. Elisha *crosses the Jordan.* There is a little phrase now occurs three times in quick succession, in verses 6 and 7 and 8. Note it well. It is the little couplet, *"They two"*, i.e. Elijah and Elisha. Master and servant now got away from all others, and went on *alone*, to the Jordan. It always has to come to that. You and I have to break away from all others, and get *alone* with our Lord Jesus. We have to go on with Him *alone* to the Jordan. See verse 6: "And he (Elisha) said: As the Lord liveth, and as thy soul liveth, I will not leave thee: so *THEY TWO WENT ON.*" See verse 7: "And fifty men of the sons of the prophets stood to view afar off (there are always many to do that and prophesy failure!) and *THEY TWO STOOD BY JORDAN.*" See verse 8: "And Elijah took his mantle, and wrapped it together, and smote the waters, and they were divided hither and thither, so that *THEY TWO WENT OVER* on dry ground."

It is *there,* on the further side of Jordan that the big thing happens! But why? It is because of what the Jordan typifies. In most of our hymns which refer to the Jordan, that ancient river is likened to death, that is, the death of the body, when the soul of the believer departs from earth to heaven. But in Old Testament typology that is never the meaning. Nay, the river Jordan typifies *our union with Christ in HIS death.*

Now remember that our Lord's Calvary death was His supreme choice of the Father's will. The same epistle which speaks about "the power of His resurrection" tells us the meaning of the Cross as it expresses our Lord's own will and choice: "He humbled Himself, and *BECAME OBEDIENT* unto death, even the death of the *CROSS"* (Phil. ii. 8). It was the supreme crisis in which He said, "Not My will, but Thine be done" (Luke xxii. 42). Even so, Jordan, which typifies our union with Him in *His* death, means the soul-crisis in which we say our deep and determined "NO" to the self-life, and our uttermost "YES" of loving abandonment to *Him.* Henceforth our motto is: The will of Christ; nothing more; nothing less; nothing else; at all costs.

That is Jordan. It is not easy. Sometimes the brink of that river is a garden of struggle and tears and sweat; for our innate "selfism" wrestles against us to the very last throw. Then, when we step into the water, we think the deep water will overflow us; and however willing we are, we shrink with fear. But no; as soon as we really take the step, the waters divide. As it was with Elisha, so it is with ourselves; we find firm footing beneath us, and go through with our Master on dry ground!

But see what happens *now!* As soon as ever Elijah and Elisha are across that Jordan, Elijah turns to Elisha and says, *"Ask what I shall do for thee, before I be taken away from thee."* What it was not possible to give on the other side, it is possible to give on this side. The type-implication is startling and thrilling. As soon as you and I are really through the Jordan with our Lord, One greater than Elijah says to us: *"Ask what ye will, and it shall be done unto you."* How many Christian believers wonder why their prayers are not answered, when all the time it is because they are praying on the wrong side of Jordan! If only our Master can get us with glad willingness through that river, on to spiritual resurrection-ground, He then says, "Ask, and ye shall receive, that your joy may be full" (John xvi. 24),—for *our* wills have become one with *His*, and His will is perfect.

Well, as soon as Elijah so spoke to Elisha, the latter was ready with his request. "I pray thee, *Let a double portion of thy spirit be upon me*" (verse 9). Elisha, who had nothing like the rugged constitution of Elijah, felt that to carry on his master's witness he would need twice as much of the Spirit as had rested on Elijah; so he asks for a "double portion" of the Spirit. It was not just an anointing, but a *fulness* of enduement for which he was earnestly applying. To this Elijah replied: "Thou hast asked a hard thing: *nevertheless*[1] if thou see me when I am taken from thee, it shall be so unto thee; but if not, it shall not be so" (verse 10). It was only a "hard thing" in the sense that Elijah himself could not *transfer* the Spirit to Elisha—not until he should transfer his *mantle* on ascending to heaven. So he adds, "If thou see me when I am taken from thee it shall be so unto thee."

After that reply, Elisha never lets his eye get away from his master. When Elijah walks *this* way, Elisha follows, *watching*; and when Elijah walks *that* way, Elisha follows, *watching*. Paul has the same intensity of focus when he says in Philippians iii. 10, "That I may know HIM, and the power of His resurrection." So must you and I fix our eyes on "Jesus only" for the blessing, once we have crossed that Jordan.

But now see what happens to Elisha. Suddenly, with breath-taking swiftness, a chariot of fire swoops down in a whirlwind, sundering the two men, and conveying Elijah upwards into space. Elisha sees the flaming horses leaping skywards, gasps in amazement, and then cries out, "My father! my father! the chariot of Israel, and the horsemen thereof!" Just a few electric seconds, and the terrific spectacle vanishes into blank space. But, look! —descending through the air . . . the mantle of Elijah!—even "the mantle of Elijah which *fell* from him"! (verse 13). That mantle is now *Elisha's*. Yes, and with it, Elisha *has the blessing*! The Spirit which rested on Elijah now rests on Elisha! (verse 15). The enduement, the "double portion" of the Spirit, is his at last!

What does Elisha do *now*? Does he say, "Oh, this is wonder-

---

[1] The word "nevertheless" does not come in the Hebrew. That is why it is printed in italics in A.V. It should be omitted, for it gives a quite wrong complexion to Elijah's reply.

ful! At last I have this wonder-working mantle. Will someone steal it from me if I go back to Jericho and Bethel? Or what if I should lose it in one of the cities? Perhaps I had better stay here. I will build a booth in this secluded place away from the madding throng, and become a monk"? Does he speak so? Far from it! See verse 13: "He took up the mantle of Elijah that fell from him, *and went back.*" Yes, he went back to those awkward folk who had sought to discourage him; back to those spiteful young men who were going to fling the sarcastic epithet at him; back to those apostate leaders and people of Israel; back to many a temptation and trial and danger. It was the exact opposite of what I read recently in a medical book on the nervous system. The nerve specialist's word was: "Finally, in most cases, to ensure permanency of the cure, the patient should not be allowed to return to the surroundings connected with his former diseased nervous state." How many of us fall into the mistaken supposition that the best way of keeping a blessing is to avoid the places where it will be tested! Our idea is that *we* must somehow preserve *it,* instead of allowing *it* to transform *us*!

Yes, Elisha went back. See what happened. Three great differences appear in him. First: *the Jordan was no longer any problem.* Verses 13 and 14 say, "He went back and stood by the bank of Jordan; and he took the mantle of Elijah that fell from him, and smote the waters, and said: Where is the Lord God of Elijah? And when he also had smitten the waters, they parted hither and thither; and Elisha went over." The new blessing was working! So is it with you and me when once we have crossed that Jordan of utter yielding to the will of our Lord Jesus. Any further going through, any subsequent call to renunciation, is easy after that decisive first crossing. We *know* those waters now! Once they were scaring to us; but now they part "hither and thither". Many other things, too, which were difficult before, now become easy.

Second; other believers now recognised in Elisha a *new spiritual quality*. Verse 15 says, "And when the sons of the prophets which were at Jericho saw him, they said: The Spirit of Elijah doth rest on Elisha!" Moreover they recognised in him a new spiritual leadership, for the verse continues, "And they came to meet him, and bowed themselves to the ground before him." We are not all called to be leaders, preachers, missionaries, or full-time Christian workers; but *whoever* we may be, when we have crossed that Jordan and have received that enduement of "power from on high" (Luke xxiv. 49), there comes a new quality in our life which is surely recognised by others. Especially if we *are* Christian ministers, preachers, or leaders of any kind, we need that experience and equipment, for there can be little vital effectiveness without it.

Third; from now onwards Elisha's ministry was one of *life-communicating resurrection-energy*. As we said earlier, this is how it all began. Elisha now moves before us as a *type* to the people of Christ of what it means to live in "the power of His resurrection". All the time we read of Elisha's exploits we should bear that in mind, for he thus becomes endlessly significant. For instance, how different he was from Elijah temperamentally and socially! Elijah was the ascetic, rough-clad, dervish-looking kind of prophet, who loved the solitudes of the hills and the open country; whereas Elisha was a townsman, a friendly mixer, a man of social habits. Oh, how we need consecrated, Spirit-filled Elishas today in our towns and cities, in our markets and ware-houses, in our offices and schools and town-councils! Oh, how all of us who love the Lord Jesus should seek to *be* His present-day Elishas! If we have followed this study of Elisha carefully, then at any rate we know *the way into* this living in the power of our Lord's resurrection. We must be true believers, living the separated life, and actively serving Christ. We must exercise faith for the further, bigger blessing. We must cross the Jordan, and receive that falling mantle, the enduing of the Spirit. It is *then* that our living in "the power of His resurrection" becomes a reality such as we have not known before.

Just one final word, maybe, is needed. There is *no* blessing of the Christian life which can be continuingly enjoyed without a regularly maintained habit of prayer and poring over the inspired pages of Holy Writ. That is why many spiritual crises prove evanescent. Prayer and the Word are air and food to spiritual life. On the other hand, crises of blessing develop into life-long enrichments as we become men and women of habitual prayer, and lovers of the Word. Oh, that you and I, having crossed our Jordan and received that mantle of enduement from on high, may continually live and work in "the power of His resurrection"! Let each one of us ask: *Am I over that Jordan?*

THE FELLOWSHIP OF HIS SUFFERINGS

I walked a mile with Pleasure.
  She chattered all the way,
But left me none the wiser
  For all she had to say.

I walked a mile with Sorrow;
  And ne'er a word spake she;
But oh, the things I learned from her,
  When Sorrow walked with me!

Robert Browning Hamilton.

THE FELLOWSHIP OF HIS SUFFERINGS

". . . And the fellowship of His sufferings, being made conformable unto His death."—Phil. iii. 10.

THE old Israelite tabernacle in the wilderness was in three parts: the "outer court", the "holy place", and the "holy of holies". Somehow, Paul's words in Philippians iii. 10 always remind me of it, for they seem to express a similar threefold progress— (1) "That I may know Him"; (2) "And the power of His resurrection"; (3) "And the fellowship of His sufferings". *All* the tabernacle was holy ground, and glorious with rich meanings; yet all led to that supremely sacred inmost shrine, the "holy of holies". Even so is it in our union with the Son of God. Sanctifying and transforming as it is to "know Him", and the "power of His resurrection", yet the holy of holies is the *"fellowship of His sufferings"*.

Years ago, soon after my conversion to Christ, I dared to suppose (with the audacity of immaturity!) that in Philippians iii. 10, our apostle had inadvertently slipped into an erroneous transposition of sequence. I thought that what he *ought* to have written was, "That I may know Him, and the fellowship of His sufferings, and *(then)* the power of His resurrection." It seemed to me that if he had written the verse in *that* order, it would have corresponded with the fact that our Lord's sufferings came first, and His resurrection afterward. I said to myself: Surely we are first to know *"Him"*, the personal Jesus who taught and wrought as shown in the four Gospels. Then we are to stand before the Cross, and see Him there in His *"sufferings"* as our Saviour. Then we are to know Him as the risen One who lives in our hearts, thus proving "the power of His *resurrection"*. I thought, too, that if only Paul had written Philippians iii. 10 in *my* amended order, it would have preserved the proper parallel with his baptismal formula in Romans vi. 4, 5, "We are buried with Him by baptism unto

death, that like as Christ was raised up from the dead by the glory
of the Father, even so we also should walk in newness of life.
For if we have been planted together in the likeness of His death,
we shall be also in the likeness of His resurrection."

Well, that certainly *is* the order in which we become the saved
people of Christ. We must first believingly accept the redemptive
meaning of His Calvary sufferings before we can be "raised up"
from spiritual death by the quickening power of His resurrection.
And the baptismal formula, too, is obviously right; for the
representative submergence of the *old* life in that liquid burial
must precede the symbolical rising in *new* life with Christ.

What, then, of Philippians iii. 10, where Paul puts the "power
of His resurrection" before the "fellowship of His sufferings"?
Why, of course, Paul is right there, too; and my own immature
notion of incorrect order was just a novice's blunder. In this
Philippian verse Paul is not thinking of the order in which we
savingly *appropriate* Christ at the *beginning* of our Christian
life, but of the way in which we *subsequently* learn to know Him
in a heart-to-heart sympathy. The key-word to our understanding
of Philippians iii. 10 is that word, "fellowship". What Paul
coveted to know was "the *fellowship* of His sufferings". Now
when you and I first came into saving union with the Son of God,
we certainly needed to know the meaning of His "sufferings"
before we could know the meaning of His "resurrection"; but in
what sense did we then come to know His "sufferings"? It certainly was not with any view to having "*fellowship*" with Him
in His sufferings. No such thought entered our minds. We came
to that Cross because the Spirit of God had made us realise what
desperately guilty, needy sinners we were; and as we stood
before the crucified Lord, the eyes of our understanding were
supernaturally enlightened to see the *sin-bearing vicariousness*
of His "sufferings". We saw that those divine-human sufferings
were mediatorially meritorious on our behalf; that they effected
a propitiation for our sin, a reconciliation with God, a redemption
from the curse of the broken law, and an eternal deliverance
from the damnation of Gehenna. Oh, how wonderful that Cross
became! But the outstanding wonder of it to us *then* was its
appropriable *substitutionariness*.

Here, however, in Philippians iii. 10, the apostle would fain
enter this holy of holies, "the *fellowship* of His sufferings". He

wanted not only to know *"Him"*, personally, directly, increasingly, and to live in the liberating "power of His resurrection", but to know Him in what must surely be the closest and deepest of all possible ways—"the fellowship of His sufferings". Moreover, Paul's very purpose in writing to tell this to us is that *you and I,* also, should covet to know our dear Lord in that inmost way.

That, of course, raises for us the crucial question: What is *meant* by "the fellowship of His sufferings", and how can *we* ever enter that holy of holies?

What this Fellowship is Not

Let us agree at once that it absolutely cannot mean any kind of *contributory* participation in His *atoning* sufferings. So far as the atoning values of His cross are concerned, our infinite Lord necessarily suffered in a solitary isolation which no finite mind can ever penetrate, let alone augment. "I have trodden the winepress alone; and of the people there was none with Me" (Isa. lxiii. 3). When Jesus entered the Garden of Gethsemane, eight of the apostles must be left at the gate; and even Peter, James, and John could not come within a stone's throw of His awesome agony. That "cup" must be drunk alone, and drained to the dregs, with not a drop left for any other.

Equally dogmatically we may say that "the fellowship of His sufferings" cannot mean any *present-day* repetitive sharing in His *historical* sufferings. Those sufferings which He endured when He was locally on this earth, two thousand years ago, are ended and gone for ever. Their terminus was announced when our Lord cried out from the Cross, "It is finished", and then yielded up His spirit. Those sufferings were as final as the atonement which they effected. They are not repeatable today for us to share in, nor can you or I go back in history two thousand years to share them as they actually occurred.

Nor again does the "fellowship of His sufferings" mean that I can somehow participate by *re-enacting* them in my *imagination*. I have known intensely emotional Christian believers express their love for Christ by trying to experience with Him, in imagination, His Calvary agonies. They have lingered over the Gospel narratives of the crucifixion, devotedly dwelling on the details, and endeavouring, in passionate adoration, to enter into the exquisite pain of it all. I have known of Roman Catholics who have even torn the skin of their palms with iron nails, and pressed thorns on their heads till the scalp bled, in their effort to enter realistically into the crucifixion agonies. Undoubtedly there is a place for soul-subduing contemplation of our Saviour's sufferings; and we moderns have need to relearn that fact from the Christians of earlier days; yet such behaviour as I have just described, however well-meaning it may be, is pathetically misguided.

The famous Saint Francis of Assisi, it is said, spent so much time mystically contemplating the Cross that after one of his protracted seasons of prayer there actually appeared in his hands the marks of crucifixion—a reproduction of our Lord's own wounds, which he carried to the day of his death. If the marks were really there, however, as is claimed, I suspect they were psycho-pathetically produced; for the strange effect of strong auto-suggestion on different parts of the body is now a scientifically demonstrable and medically accepted phenomenon. But with all respect to Saint Francis, *that* is far from what Paul had in mind when he wrote, "That I may know Him . . . and the fellowship of His sufferings."

What this Fellowship Is

What, then, *does* this "fellowship of His sufferings" mean? Well, first, it means that we may enter *sympathetically* into our Saviour's Calvary sufferings, even though they are long past. Although those actual sufferings are now over, the same *feelings* are still in His heart as were there *then*. Remember, even though His crucifixion was a gory spectacle of shame and torture, His physical sufferings were the *least* of His sufferings. Those of His soul and spirit were measurelessly deeper—though in saying this we are far from minimising the physical. We may feelingly enter into His spurned and cruelly ill-requited love, His yearning, unquenchable compassion for the race which was repudiating Him, His costly self-denial; His meek submission, His heart-brokenness over the sin and sorrows of the world, His unflinching master-purpose to do the Father's will. Our Saviour's heart is still the same; so that therefore, by a grateful heart-to-heart fellowship with Him, I may *sympathetically,* even though only retrospectively, enter into those *inward* sufferings which He ever remembers, and into those underlying emotions and compassions which still live on in His heart.

Quite recently a lovely illustration of this came to my notice, in Winnipeg, Canada. When in the company of our elderly friend, Mr. Hugh L. MacKinnon, a beloved Christian leader of that city, we observed a photograph between the pages of his Bible. It turned out to be a picture of his saintly father, now long since gone to be "at home with the Lord". Mr. MacKinnon explained that the photograph was always kept there—between the same two pages, at the fifty-third chapter of Isaiah, because the dear old father so loved that chapter, and so often read it with his children, but could *never* read it without *breaking into tears*! Each time he read it, he so sympathetically entered into the anguish of the Saviour he loved, and was so overcome by grateful marvelling at the love which poured itself out on Calvary, that his feelings overcame him, and his eyes became fountains of tears. Yes, indeed, we may know "the fellowship of His sufferings" in *that* way!

But again, the "fellowship of His sufferings" means that we may enter sympathetically into His *present* sufferings. Does it come as a surprise to someone that our exalted Lord should have "present" sufferings? Yet can it be otherwise? I know that there must be an unimaginably felicitous joy in His heart as He reigns in the pure glory of His heavenly exaltation. What rapture of repose and reward must be His in the love and honour of the Father, whose will He perfectly accomplished "even to the death of the Cross"! What joy as He retrospectively contemplates His finished work of atonement! What joy amid the presence and adoring gratitude of His redeemed people, so many of whom are now gathered yonder with Him! What joy is His in those unfallen angel-spirits whose utter bliss is to do the bidding of their lovely King! What joy in anticipation of the coming consummation when, with Satan and sin finally abolished, He shall reign in the New Jerusalem "unto the ages of the ages"! Yes, what joy! Yet it does not exclude other emotions from His infinite heart. Does not the world which crucified Him still reject Him? Do not millions and millions worship false gods, and grope in darkness amid Satanically inflicted deceptions? Are not His own people on earth penalised and persecuted? Does He not grieve with the Father over the perishing? Does He not suffer with His suffering people on earth?

Remember, when our risen Lord suddenly intercepted the fulminating anti-Nazarene Saul of Tarsus on the road to Damascus, He called down, "Saul, Saul, why persecutest thou *Me?*" It was not, "Why persecutest thou *them?*" but "Why persecutest thou *ME?*" Every blow which was falling on them was felt by *Him!* Every lash which whipped their backs cut into *Him!* In the words of Isaiah lxiii. 9, "In all *their* afflictions *He* was afflicted." The intensity of our Lord's feelings is indicated in the twice-uttered name, "Saul, Saul. . . ." Moreover, as He felt with His people on earth *then,* so does He *now,* for in the words of Hebrews iv. 15, our dear High Priest in heaven is "*touched* with the feeling of *our* infirmities".

Into all these present sufferings of our Lord—His sufferings over an impenitent Christendom, over millions who grope in heathen darkness, over multitudes that are perishing, over the godly who are afflicted, over the declension of the organised church, and especially His sufferings with His own elect people —into all these you and I may sympathetically enter, if we live in heart-to-heart communion with Him, even as Paul did when in carrying "the care of all the churches", he wrote to the Corinthians, "Who is weak, and *I* am not weak? Who is offended, and *I* burn not?" (2 Cor. xi. 29). Indeed, he had so entered into the feelings of Christ that he could write in Philippians i. 8, "I long after you all *in the very compassions* of Jesus Christ." When we are sympathetically one with our Lord to that degree, we have undoubtedly entered into "the fellowship of His sufferings".

Still further, we begin to know "the fellowship of His sufferings" when we willingly undergo the *same kind* of sufferings as He endured in "the days of His flesh". Those Christians who relax principle or stifle testimony to evade being ostracised, stigmatised, or otherwise penalised, may escape discomforts to the flesh, but oh, how they miss the deeper, richer joys of fellowship with their Lord! We never quite so vividly enjoy His soul-thrilling companionship as when we endure the same kind of sufferings for Him as He endured for us.

Think, for instance, of His self-denial. He had fasted for "forty days and forty nights" when Satan first came out openly to tempt Him. Was His fast a total abstention from food? It is difficult to think of anyone, after such a fast, retaining sufficient self-command to undergo such an encounter, unless body and brain were under the control of a supernormally strong mind. This much is certain: our Saviour must have been physically much reduced, and tortured with hunger-pangs (Matt. iv. 2). Indeed, that is why the tempter came out *then*, and with apparent sympathy suggested that if Jesus was indeed "the Son of God", then obviously He should at once exercise His divine power to transmute stones into bread, and thereby appease His raging human hunger. Let us have no doubt, our Master's hunger-pains must have been acutely real, and the soft-toned solicitation of Satan was disarmingly subtle, but Jehovah's perfect Servant would sooner starve to death inside the will of God than feed and live outside it; so He says "No" to His human nature, even though the appeasing of its hunger was something perfectly innocent in itself. So it was all the way onward; He said an equally unbending "No" to self, and an equally unflinching "Yes" to God, until at last, in that critical wrestle and sweat of Gethsemane, He blended the two extremes of utter pain and utter joy in the cry, "Not My will; but Thine!"

Even so, when you and I, in approximate measure, begin to say the same kind of "No" to self and "Yes" to Him, we enter that holy of holies, "the fellowship of His sufferings". It is never easy to the flesh, though each victory over the flesh makes the next one easier; and the lovely paradox is that the harder the victory the more thrilling is *His* fellowship with *us* and *our* fellowship with *Him*!

Our Lord had to endure the hatred of the religious professionalists; the scorn of the intellectual aristocracy; the misunderstanding of His kindred; the contemptuous repudiation of His townsmen; the deceitful intrigue of hypocritical friends and foes; the rejection of His message by a fickle populace; hunger, thirst, weariness, disappointment, ill-treatment, unfair trial, blows, whippings, mockings, crucifixion, death. ("Blessed be His glorious Name for ever"!) And whenever you and I willingly endure any such sufferings for *His* sake, we find ourselves entering "the fellowship of His sufferings". Suddenly in the seven-times-heated furnace "One like the Son of God" walks and talks with us amid the flames!

What Then of Ourselves?

What then of ourselves? To what degree do you and I know "the fellowship of His sufferings"? Let us sum up what we have been saying, and then test ourselves somewhat. To dwell in "the fellowship of His sufferings" is to share *sympathetically* those feelings and compassions and inward sufferings which not only were in His heart when He suffered on Calvary but are still in His heart continuingly. It is to suffer as He suffered, and still suffers, in the afflictions of His people. It is to find our hearts grieving with *His* heart over the sinning, sorrowing Christless millions. It is the wonderful fellowship of intimate, reciprocal sympathy between Him and us when for His dear sake we willingly endure the *same kind* of sufferings as *He* suffered for *us*. It is saying the same kind of "No" to the "self" as He said, even though it means an *inward* crucifixion corresponding to His *outward* crucifixion. This is not easy. It is sometimes excruciating indeed to the "self" and the "flesh"; yet it somehow opens the gates into the purest ecstasy we can experience this side of heaven!

Now, are you and I really *willing* to enter "the fellowship of His sufferings"? It is the way by which we come to know our Lord best of all; but are we really willing? This is the way into the richest joy of all; but are we really willing? This is the inner circle of communion with Heaven which, in our heart of hearts, we *desire* more than all; but are we really willing? Are we willing to make more time for secret waiting in His presence? Are we willing to linger there for as many hours as we spend on less-important and sometimes trivial things? We may settle it once for all in our minds: it is only the prayerful who are privileged to share closely the companionship of His heart. Are you and I willing to wait on Him often enough and long enough for Him to impress his mind upon ours, so that His mind thinks through ours, and His feelings communicate themselves through ours, and His compassions flow through ours, enlarging them into His own boundless sympathies? Do we realise that prayer-sharing with Him is the *incomparable* privilege? Are we willing, nay, determined to give prayer first place?

Are we willing, also, to suffer for His sake the same kind of sufferings as *He* suffered for *our* sake? When persecution or other kind of penalty attends our witness for Him, do we bear it in a spirit like that of the flogged apostles who "departed from the presence of the council rejoicing that they were counted worthy to suffer shame for His name"? (Acts v. 41). Or do we dodge such humiliations, with fond respect for the safety of our own skin? Am I willing, with Paul, to "bear in my body the *brands* of the Lord Jesus" (Gal. vi. 17)?

In a revival meeting some time ago a crowd of Christians were lustily singing the well-known hymn,

> Will there be any stars, any stars in my crown,
> When at evening the sun goeth down?

In that meeting a friend of mine happened to be near an aged Christian brother who kept singing it (either by choice or through defective vision),

> Will there be any *scars*, any *scars* in my crown,
> When at evening the sun goeth down?

Are you and I willing for "scars" as well as "stars"? How Paul rebukes most of us in this matter! "In stripes above measure, in prisons more frequent, in deaths oft. Of the Jews five times received I forty stripes save one. Thrice was I beaten with rods, once was I stoned, thrice I suffered shipwreck, a night and a day I have been in the deep. In journeyings often, in perils of waters, in perils of robbers, in perils by mine own countrymen, in perils by the heathen, in perils in the city, in perils in the wilderness, in perils in the sea, in perils among false brethren, in weariness and painfulness, in watchings often, in hunger and thirst, in fastings often, in cold and nakedness. Beside those things that are without, that which cometh upon me daily, the care of all the churches" (2 Cor. xi. 23–28).

Let us face up to a further test. Are you and I willing to carry a *burden* for souls?—rather, are we willing to share *His* compassionate concern for the perishing until it really hurts? Did you ever read *Down in Water Street*? It is no longer new, but what a story it is, of wonderful conversions and transformations among drunkards and criminals! Sam Hadley, its author, was perhaps the most remarkable case of all. What a soul-winner he became, in and through that Water Street Mission! Let me tell you something about that same Sam Hadley which I learned from the late Dr. Henry Montgomery of Belfast, Northern Ireland.

Years ago, when he (Dr. Montgomery) was in New York with Charles M. Alexander, the well-known song-leader in the Torrey-Alexander evangelistic campaigns, Mr. Alexander asked Sam Hadley if he would take him to see some of the night dens of New York, so that he might have a clearer idea of what went on in the city during the night. The two of them started at twelve midnight. At 2 a.m. Mr. Alexander had become so sickened by what he had seen that he needed to call off. He left Sam Hadley at a street corner, but after walking away a few paces he heard Hadley's uneven limp stop, and on looking round saw him leaning heavily against a lamp-post, his head resting wearily on his arm. Mr. Alexander hurried back, thinking his friend was ill; but as he drew nearer, he heard Sam Hadley sob, *"Oh, God . . . oh, God . . . the sin of this city is breaking my heart!"* Have you and I entered into "the fellowship of His sufferings" to such a degree as that?

F. W. H. Myer, in his famous poem, "St. Paul", has vividly depicted the same upsurge of sympathy and passion in the great apostle.

"Only like souls I see the folk thereunder,
　　Bound who should conquer, slaves who should be kings,—
Hearing their one hope with an empty wonder,
　　Sadly contented in a show of things;—

Then with a rush the intolerable craving
　　Shivers throughout me like a trumpet call,—
Oh to save these! to perish for their saving,
　　Die for their life, be offered for them all!

Christ! I am Christ's! and let the name suffice you,
　　Aye, for me too He greatly hath sufficed:
Lo with no winning words I would entice you,
　　Paul has no honour and no friend but Christ."

We find the same in noble-hearted Jeremiah. "Oh, that my head were waters, and mine eyes a fountain of tears, that I might weep day and night for the slain of the daughter of my people." "Mine heart within me is broken because of the prophets. All my bones shake; I am like a drunken man, and like a man whom wine hath overcome" (ix. 1; xxiii. 9).

All Scottish Christians of the last generation were proud of their great evangelist, the Rev. John McNeill. Not so many have heard of his big-hearted son, the Rev. Archie McNeill, who, alas, was killed in a road accident near Portland, Oregon, some years ago. Archie's brave widow told me that when he and she used to pray together or with groups of believers, he could never pray for the unsaved without breaking down and weeping. Do you and I feel and pray like *that*?

Or, again, we may test ourselves by asking: Am I living in such community of feeling with Christ that everything which hurts the *other* members of His mystic body and bride, the Church, pains *me*? Am I sympathetically one with the *spiritual* Zion as Nehemiah was with the earthly, when on hearing of its broken walls and burned gates he "wept, and mourned, and fasted, and prayed before the God of heaven" (Neh. i. 4)? Am I as sensitively one with true believers of *my* day as Paul was with *his* day, when he wrote, "Who is weak, and I am not weak? Who is offended, and I burn not" (2 Cor. xi. 29)?

Let no one think that there is even the faintest streak of morbidity in these self-interrogations. This entering into "the fellowship of His sufferings" of which we are speaking is *utterly* removed from gloomy broodings and sanctimonious mopings. Those men and women who have most deeply entered into this inner union of mind with the holy Son of God have always been men and women of much prayer, but they have seldom if ever been cloistered recluses or monastic mystics detached from the real world of everyday work and play. None was ever holier than our Lord Jesus, yet none was ever a better mixer. None was ever more uncompromisingly removed from guile and wrong, yet none was ever more practically in touch with human need. None ever bore so great a burden of sorrow, yet none ever had such rich and quenchless joy—a joy so high and deep that even on the way to the ordeal of Gethsemane, Gabbatha, and Golgotha, He could say, "These things have I spoken unto you that *My joy* might remain in you" (John xv. 11). Contradictory as it may seem to a merely "natural" mind, this "fellowship of His sufferings" is the hidden door to inward joy and outward radiance.

> We never know real joy until we suffer.
> We never really laugh until we really weep.
> We never know the sweet but by the bitter,
> And all who sow in tears rich harvest reap.

I suppose there has never been a mightier preacher of the Gospel than the famous Charles Hadden Spurgeon. Besides being a prince of preachers, he was a great humorist. I doubt whether there ever was a man of more bubbling good humour than he. Yet how he entered into the fellowship of his Master's suffering! Once when I was just a young preacher I ministered at a certain fashionable church in London, and expatiated on the text, "What must I do to be saved?" Afterwards, a retired old Baptist minister came to me and introduced himself as "one of the first six students C. H. Spurgeon took in to his newly-opened Pastor's College fifty years ago." He then said, "How the dear guv'nor would have thrilled to hear you tonight!" To which I replied, "No, sir; if the great C. H. S. had been here, *I* should have been stepping down to hear *him*". This quite annoyed the dear old minister. "No, no, my young friend!" he exclaimed. "You have never known him as *we* did. If the guv'nor had been here, he would have been sitting in that corner over there; and while you were preaching, the sweat would have dripped down his face as he prayed for the power of God to save souls through your preaching!" Do you and I blend such good humour and such spiritual intensity as that?

Well, there it is, this strangest of all paradoxes: richest joy by deepest sorrow; out of the bitter flows sweetness; the cross is a latent throne; tears become windows into heaven; the deeper we go, the higher we rise; and self-abnegation for others is the golden portal to highest self-fulfilment. The nearer we get to Christ, the more we enter the love-secret which turns sighs into songs, weights into wings, burdens into blessings, and crucifixions into coronations.

> Then let me not shudder to tread even there,
> His awful Gethsemane night-gloom to share;
> For there I am nearest the deeps of His love,
> And *they* are the *joy*-springs of heaven above!

CONFORMITY TO CALVARY

Higher than the highest heaven,
Deeper than the deepest sea,
Lord, Thy love at last hath conquered ;
Grant me now my heart's desire,
None of self, and all of Thee.

Theodore Monod.

CONFORMITY TO CALVARY

"Being made conformable unto His death"—Phil. iii. 10.

THIS is the spiritual ultimate on which Paul's heart is set. He must go the whole way. He must follow out the pattern to the last strand. He must not only "know" Christ in a living fellowship, and in "the power of His resurrection", and in "the fellowship of His sufferings", he must even be "made conformable unto His death".

Instead of the words "made conformable", however, it is better to read, "becoming conformed", for the Greek participle here (see English Revised and American Standard Version) implies continuity, development, progress.

"Being conformed unto His death." Let it be emphasized again that Paul did not mean any mere *physical* conformity, a being crucified bodily after the pattern of Calvary. No, He wanted to live in the *spirit* of Calvary, in the attitude of utter love-obedience to God, and self-denying love to men. The base of the Greek participle is *morphe*, which means "form", as in Philippians ii. 6, 7. We get our modern word "morphosis" from it. Paul wanted to be changed by an inward and spiritual "metamorphosis" into the fullest possible likeness to the Christ of Calvary.

So, then, we take a parting look at Philippians iii. 10, noting that when Paul longs more fully to know the fellowship of our Lord's sufferings, it was that he might now become *"conformed unto His death"*. In this Philippian epistle the aspect of our Lord's death which is given prominence is that of His *obedience* to the Father. "He became obedient unto death, even the death of the Cross." Paul longs to know "the fellowship of His sufferings" to the point where his own obedience to the divine will is the nearest possible replica of that perfect pattern. In other words, he wants this fellowship in His Master's sufferings to effect a transformation in the deepest reaches of his *character*, so that he too, like "the Captain of our salvation", might be made "perfect through sufferings" (Heb. ii. 10).

That is of highest significance. There is coming an hour when all the blood-bought, Spirit-born people of Christ will be presented "faultless before the throne of His glory with exceeding joy" (Jude 24). We shall then have sinless hearts and perfected powers; that is, we shall be perfect in our *nature*. But does that perfection of *nature* mean that we shall then all be alike in qualities of *character*? No; the sufferings and experiences of this present life on earth (or rather our *reactions* to them) are doing something in our *character* which will endure in the Beyond, fitting us (if we rightly react to them) for special ministries in that destiny through "the ages to come". The stars may all be made of the same material, but "one star differeth from another star in glory" (1 Cor. xv. 41)—that is, they are the same in nature, but they differ in character! "If we *suffer*, we shall also *reign* with Him" (2 Tim. ii. 12)—and the way we suffer may determine the way we reign!

This leads us at once to see the gracious purpose which may lie underneath many of the sicknesses and other sorrows which are divinely permitted in human life on earth. Here is one who is crippled from cradle to grave. Here is another who is bedfast with an incurable malady for weary years. How we might extend such instances! And how baffling they seem! Does God really love them? Is He being cruel? Why such enigmas? But perhaps they are only baffling because we are blind! Listen: two thousand years ago, a bedraggled beggar sat by a roadside in Palestine—blind, ignorant, and unheeded by most of the busy passers-by. The disciples asked Jesus, "Master, who did sin, this man or his parents, that he was born blind?" And Jesus gave the fathomless reply, "Neither hath this man sinned, nor his parents; *but that the works of God should be made manifest in him*" (John ix. 2, 3). Think of it: that insignificant, anonymous, blind beggar, in the thought and purpose of God before time was, and predestined to be at that roadside when Jesus walked there, so that "the works of God should be made manifest in him" by the sight-giving miracle which Jesus now performed (verses 4–7), and that the man's soul should thereby become eternally saved! (verses 35–38).

Oh, let us beware of judging God hastily! "Behind a frowning providence He hides a smiling face." God help us to react believingly and resignedly to permitted suffering. It may be heaven's sweetest angel visiting us in disguise. It can achieve qualities in our *character*, and fit us for high *destiny*, as perhaps nothing else can! Paul well knew this when he said, "That I may know Him . . . and the fellowship of His sufferings".

How many saintly sufferers have discovered this character-developing purpose in their sufferings! Take the following witness from the matured wisdom of Annie Johnson Flint, after incurable illness, and daily recurrence of acute pain. Only once did she turn from the poet's muse to prose; and outside of Bunyan's *Pilgrim's Progress,* scarcely can a more telling allegory ever have been written.

And it came to pass, as I travelled along the Highway of Life, that I saw in the distance, far ahead, a mountain, and on it One standing, upon whose face rested a divine compassion for the grief of the world.

His raiment was white and glittering, and in His hand was a cross. And He called unto the sons of men, saying, "Come! Come! Who will take up his cross and follow Me, that he may be like unto Me, and that I may seat him at my right hand and share with him things glorious and beautiful beyond the dreams of earth and the imaginings of men?"

And I said, "What is my cross that I may take it up?"

And a Voice answered, "There are many crosses, and thine shall be given thee in good time."

And I said, "What will bring me near to Thee and make me most like Thee?"

And the Voice replied, "There are many angels with whom thou canst walk; but see that they lead thee only toward Me, and never away from Me, for some there be that will cause thee to forget Me."

And I said, "What angel shall be given me?" And I felt a hand laid upon mine, and saw beside me one with a smiling face, who said, "Walk with me; I am the Angel of Joy."

Then all my life grew bright, and wealth was mine, and many pleasures, and friends crowded around me, and Love crowned me, and I knew no care.

But suddenly I heard the Voice, and it sounded faint and far off, and it said, "Alas! Thou art not coming toward Me." And I fell upon my knees, crying, "Oh, forgive me that I could forget Thee! Take away the angel, since he leads me not unto Thee."

Then the world grew dark, and I heard a low voice beside me saying, "Come with me; I am the Angel of Sorrow."

Then he took my hand in his, and I went with him, weeping. But now there were no friends around me, and pleasure palled upon me, and my heart was very sad. And as I went I saw that the Vision grew brighter, and I perceived that I was no longer walking away from it.

But my soul was exceeding sorrowful, and I looked back often, and saw in memory the joys I had once known, until the tears blinded me, and I stumbled continually, for the path was rough, and *it had begun to lead upward*.

Then I heard the Voice again, and it said, "Look not back; regret not the past; I will send thee another angel who will help thee to forget the things which are behind."

Then the Angel of Sorrow vanished, and in his place stood one whose face was cheerful, and he said, "Come! Let us be up and doing; I am the Angel of Work."

And I went with him—at first with lagging steps and a sore heart; but as my sight became clearer, I beheld many sick and discouraged, many who had fallen by the way. Then I heard the Voice again saying, "The labourers are few. Inasmuch as ye have done it unto the least of these, ye have done it unto Me."

So I began to help those around me, and as my hands grew busy, my heart lightened, and I forgot to look behind me and mourn for the lost joys of the past, and at times there was even a song upon my lips. But the road was rough, and often dark, and at times my courage failed me and my soul was disquieted within me; for there were sorrows I could not comfort, and hunger I could not satisfy, and burdens I could not help to lift; and I could only stretch out my hands and cry, "Oh, Thou who hast helped me, help these, for I cannot."

Then the Voice said, "Be not weary in well-doing. Thou art coming toward Me. I will send one who will bring thee still nearer."

Then I saw beside me an angel with a veil before his face, who said in a grave voice, "Canst thou walk with me? I am the Angel of Sacrifice."

But I shrank back, murmuring, "What wilt thou take from me?" And he answered, "I will take nothing. Thou must thyself give it of thine own free will. It is thy Dearest Wish."

Then I hid my face in my hands, and cried, "I cannot! I cannot! Ask me something else! Give me some task to do! Have I not laboured faithfully these many days? Did I not myself resign the joys that were once so precious to me, and turn away from them to follow Thee? And I will still follow Thee—still work for Thee, only leave me this one thing! It is so dear to me—it is my light in darkness, my food in hunger, my rest in weariness, my comfort always! Yet I have not loved it better than Thee; it has not led me away from Thee, nor hidden from me the heavenly Vision."

Then the voice said, "Thou canst do without all these things—light and food, rest and comfort; but canst thou do without Me? Thou must choose between us. Is it too hard for thee? And yet thou saidst thou wouldst be nearer me!"

Then I cried in answer, "Yes, yes, I would; but oh! is there not another way? Take all else, and leave me only this!" But the Voice spoke no more.

Then I struggled until the sweat broke out upon my brow in drops of agony, and my nights were sleepless, and my days troubled, and the Vision grew dim, and I saw no light.

But then came a day when the Higher triumphed, and with broken voice and streaming eyes, I held out my Dearest Wish, crying, "Take it, take it! Thy will be done!"

Then the Vision broke in splendour, and I heard the Voice saying, "Thou hast fought a good fight. Now thou art indeed Mine; and behold, thy reward is even now beside thee!"

So I looked, and the angel had lifted his veil and was smiling, and lo! it was the Wish I had given up, but changed—beautified and glorified, a heavenly blessing in the place of an earthly.

Then it vanished from my sight, and the Voice spoke again: "Thy sacrifice is accepted. Thou shalt see it no more on Earth; but through all the days of thy mortal pilgrimage it shall be to thee a blessed hope, and it shall meet thee at the gate of heaven, to be thine through all eternity. And thou hast come much nearer unto Me, and art more like Me. Dost thou desire to draw still nearer to me?" I cried, "Yes, yes, still nearer!" And the Voice replied, "There is but one angel more for thee to walk with. It is the Angel of Suffering."

Then a great trembling seized me and I said, "The spirit is willing, but the flesh is weak. I know not if I can endure. Yet do with me as Thou wilt, for I am Thine."

Then suddenly there appeared before me an angel whose face was lined and furrowed as with the deep strokes of a chisel, yet over all there was the beauty of a conqueror's peace—a peace wrested from great tribulation, the look of one who had forgotten how to weep.

One hand he held out to me, and with the other he pointed to the ground. And I looked and saw before me the cross which I had last seen in the hand of Him upon the Mount.

Then the Voice said, "This only is the way by which thou canst approach nearest unto Me and be most like Me. This is thy cross. Lie down upon it without shrinking and without fear. Thou shalt not be alone; I too have been there. I sounded all the depths of pain, and at the last I was forsaken by the Father; but that last, worst suffering thou shalt not know, for I will never leave thee nor forsake thee."

So I lay down upon the cross, and I rest upon it even unto this day. And the Angel of Suffering watches upon my left hand, and upon my right is One who comes along with him—the Angel of His Presence. And of late there has been another, the Angel of Peace. And the three abide always with me.

And the Vision is a vision no longer, but a Reality. And it is not a stern Judge, nor a merciful God, but a loving Father, who bends over me. The way has brought me almost to His feet. There is but a narrow valley that divides us, the Valley of the Shadow, and the angel who shall lead me through it is the Angel of Death.

I wait his coming with a tranquil heart, for beneath the mask that frights the timid human hearts which dread his summons I shall see a face I know—the face of the Son of God, who has walked beside me in the furnace of affliction, so that I passed through without even the smell of fire on my garments.

And when I go down into the deep waters, it is His arm I shall lean upon, and the voice that welcomes me upon the other side will be His.

And at the gate my guide shall leave me, and I shall see Him no more until I behold Him at the right hand of God, having upon His head many crowns, and on His vesture a name written, "King of Kings, and Lord of Lords", before whose face heaven and earth shall flee away.

And the multitude of them that are saved shall stand before Him, and they that come up out of great tribulation, who endure to the end, and inherit all things, and they shall cry with a loud voice saying, "Blessing and honour and glory and power be unto Him that sitteth upon the throne, and unto the Lamb for ever and ever."

And in Him who sitteth upon the throne I shall know the Man of Sorrows, whom I saw upon the Mount of Vision, holding in His hand a cross and calling unto the sons of men, "Come! Come! Who will take up his cross and follow Me, that he may be like unto Me, and that I may set him upon my right hand, and share with him things glorious and beautiful beyond the dreams of earth and the imaginings of men?"

Yes, that "one angel more" was needed, even the "Angel of Suffering", if there was to be complete conformity to the Christ of Calvary.

Well, so it is, that in the Pauline way or in the Annie Johnson Flint way we become "conformed unto His *death*". Paul certainly did not long to become conformed to the pattern of Calvary for the sake of some divine reward, but solely for the sake of just *being* as Christ was. That in itself was the reward, for the supreme paradox of the Christian life is that in the deepest depth we scale the highest height, and in vicarious self-sacrifice we reach victorious self-realisation. In our very cross we find our throne! It is not just that the cross leads to the throne: the cross *is* the throne; and in the very dying we find the life that is life indeed.

A certain popular advertisement has it that "Life begins at Forty". I recently saw something far truer in a minister's study: "Life begins at Calvary". The discerning eye of Paul saw right through to the truth that real life is by death—by death to selfism, and the more complete the death, the fuller the life. Oh, that you and I could see this more clearly!

Perhaps here, however, a cautionary word is needed. We have sometimes read or heard teachings on sanctification to the effect that the "self" in us must die. From that idea we surely must dissent. The "self" is the actual person, the basic, thinking *ego*; and the death of the "self", therefore, would be nothing less than the obliteration of the human personality. What the New Testament teaches is that we are to die to self*ism*, so that the whole of our personality may be interpenetrated by the life of the indwelling Christ. We are to die to egocentricity, or self-centredness. Instead of all the while living selfward, we are to live with a Christlike, sympathetic outreaching toward others. There *is* to be death to self-seeking, self-indulgence, self-sparing, and every other form of self-centredness.

That kind of death is not only possible, it is the gateway to the purest joy this side of heaven. Yes, that is really so, however difficult it may seem for some of us to grasp it. Recall, again, that Jesus was actually on the way to Gethsemane and Calvary when He said, "My *joy*", and "My *peace*". The "get-all-you-can" policy or the "give-yourself-a-good-time" spirit may seem the quick way to joy, but in reality the very opposite is true. Selfishness is ever the assassin of joy. It is only when egoism is ousted by a Christlike "otherism" that we find the secret of our Master's quenchless joy and depthless peace.

If only we had more of Paul's longing to be "conformed unto His death", we should find as he did the "joy unspeakable and full of glory". How many of the saints have found that their heavenliest joy came through their deepest sorrow or suffering! Again and again, the very calamities which have been dreaded and shunned have been permitted to overtake the apprehensive disciple; but instead of bringing the dreaded desolation they have opened the mind to joys undreamed of beforehand. I have a friend who went blind—an affliction which he had nervously dreaded. One day, after many months in the darkness, he exclaimed to me in a tone of quite rapturous confidentiality, "Man, I never really saw anything until I lost my sight!" It reminded me of Fanny Crosby, the beloved hymn-writer, who also went blind. On one occasion a friend was shown the way to her room for an appointment, and must have entered a few seconds before Miss Crosby expected. The visitor saw the blind hymn-writer slowly pacing the room, and overheard her softly exclaiming, "Wonderful! wonderful! Lord, this is wonderful! Oh, what a lot those poor people miss who can see!"

Ah, it is a true paradox—life by way of death; joy by way of sorrow; peace by way of storm; sight by way of blindness! When our Lord would lead us into the deeper things of the Spirit, sometimes He must send afflictions which seem cruel at first, to introduce us into "the fellowship of His sufferings", and thereby to "conform" us to His death. Alas, that this should be needed! Oh, to live where Theodore Monod's hymn carries us:

> Higher than the highest heaven,
> Deeper than the deepest sea,
> Lord, Thy love at last hath conquered,
> Grant me now my heart's desire,
> None of self, and *all* of Thee!

We must bring this present study to an end. In doing so let us try to bring it to a focus-point. We may concisely define our Saviour's suffering thus: It was the bearing of a special suffering which *God* laid on Him for the fulfilling of a divine purpose; and it was a suffering on behalf of *others*. Even so, when you and I for Christ's sake willingly bear a special cross which God lays on us for the proving and chastening of our hearts, and by which He may bless others through us, then, and only then, we begin to enter into a deep, sympathetic understanding of the sufferings of Christ such as we could never know otherwise, and we also find our risen Lord entering into a wondrous fellowship with *us* such as we could never know otherwise. *We* enter into *His* sufferings; and *He* enters into ours. We thus learn to know Him more closely and deeply—yes, let us say it reverently, more *affectionately*—than by any other way.

> Though a garden of Gethsemane
>   May lie athwart my way;
> Though the sorrows of a Calvary
>   May quench the light of day;
> It is there, in deepest sadness,
>   That He most transfigures pain,
> Turning grief to purest gladness,
>   Deepest loss to richest gain.

And if thereby we are made "conformable unto His *death*", think to what it ultimately leads. See the climax to which all else in the chapter leads up: "Our citizenship is in heaven; from whence also we look for the Saviour, the Lord Jesus Christ; who shall change this body of our humiliation that it may be *fashioned like unto His glorious body*." The Greek word here translated as "fashioned" is the one which in our text is rendered as "conformed".

> Verse 10: "Conformed unto His *death*."
> Verse 21: "Conformed unto His *glory*."

Let us not only say it, but really pray it:

"THAT I MAY KNOW HIM, AND THE POWER OF HIS RESURRECTION, AND THE FELLOWSHIP OF HIS SUFFERINGS, BEING MADE CONFORMABLE UNTO HIS DEATH."

Part Two: ABOUT LOVING HIM

So far, we have been speaking about knowing *Christ;* but by its very nature such a theme impels us onward to further territory. Knowing Him must be complemented by loving *Him,* for as the intellect finds in Him its supreme illumination and reward, so the heart finds in Him the perfectly delectable Object of its love. None can satisfy the outreaching of the human heart as He. The more we ponder this, the more luminous and certain it becomes. Others are but "broken lights" compared with Him. He is the sum and crown of all moral excellence, and therefore supremely loveable. It is said that "love is blind"; yet is it not they who say so who are blind? Love can see more through a tear-drop than Reason ever saw through a telescope or a microscope! To minds blinded by "the god of this age" our Lord may be merely a "root out of a dry ground", but to the opened eyes of faith and love He is "the fairest among ten thousand and the altogether lovely". Yet our love to Him must not be merely aesthetic or contemplative or sentimental; it must be the outreaching of active passion. It is in doing, not dreaming, that true love wings upward to its zenith of joy. In reality, love is not just affection, but devotion; and it reaches its highest expression, not in sympathy, but in sacrifice. True love to Christ is no mere mystical admiration, but a practical loyalty. Such love is what our Lord seeks from us more than all else. There is no substitute because there is no equivalent. Staggering though it sounds, it is true: He wants my love. When I love Him "with all my heart and mind and soul and strength", then, and only then, does it become individually true of me, "He shall see of the travail of His soul and shall be satisfied."

THE UNSEEN LOVED ONE

"Whom having not seen, ye love."—I Peter i. 8.

CONSIDERED merely grammatically, these words form a quite simple statement; but as the expression of a religious and spiritual reality they have wide and wonderful horizons. As heaven and earth are reflected in one tiny dewdrop, so here a whole world of unique meaning eradiates from this one short sentence.

1. Christianity Centres in a Person

Take that first word in the text, the pronoun,—*"Whom* having not seen, ye love." It brings home to us right away the fact that *Christianity centres in a Person.* The Christian religion does not centre in an idea, a truth, a dogma, a creed, a ritual, an office, a tradition, a system, an event, a building, a geographical Mecca. No; it centres in a Person, our Lord Jesus Christ.

Now so far as I know, that cannot be said in anything like the same way about any other religion on earth. Confucianism, if it can still be said to centre in Confucius, centres in his moral maxims rather than in his person. Buddhism revolves round a philosophic concept rather than round Gautama himself. Hinduism is a mosaic of myth and mysticism, but it centres in none of its sages, pandits or mahatmas. Even Mohammedanism, despite its fanatical homage to Mohammed, does not conceive of him as an abiding presence; it centres in the Koran rather than in the prophet himself.

Certainly, those non-Christian religions derive from real, historical, human founders, but they do not centre in them; for those founders are no longer personally necessary to the religious systems which they originated; and the systems can go on apart from them. The spider and the web are distinct from each other, and the web remains though the spider is dead. The relationship of those founders to the faiths which they originated is *not* that of the root and the flower, in which the flower is dependent for its very life on the continuance of the root. The relationship is rather that of the architect and the edifice. The architect has forever passed away, but the building, for what it is worth, lingers on.

With Christianity it is strikingly otherwise. As a great missionary has put it, "Christianity is Christ." The Christian focus-point is not what Jesus *taught*, nor even what Jesus *wrought*, though both His teaching and His atoning self-sacrifice are surpassingly sublime. The vital centre is *Jesus Himself*—the virgin-born God-Man, the sinless Exemplar, the vicarious Sin-bearer, the resurrected Saviour, the ascended Intercessor, the omnipresent Indweller of His people, and the soon-returning royal Bridegroom of His Church. Yes, Jesus Himself is the sum and substance, the centre and the very life of Christianity. Take away *Him*, and you destroy *it*.

This is the uniform emphasis of the New Testament. Paul, who was distinctively the theologian of the apostles, when he would coin a manifesto of apostolic preaching, says: "We preach not ourselves, but *Christ Jesus as Lord*" (2 Cor. iv. 5); and when he dips his quill to write a last word before his martyrdom, it is: "I know *Whom* (not merely 'what') I have believed" (2 Tim. i. 12). Similarly, John epitomises the Gospel: "This is the record: God hath given to us eternal life, and *this life is in His Son*" (1 John v. 11). So is it with Peter, as indicated in our text: "*Whom* having not seen, ye love." Yes, Christianity centres in a Person, in *that* Person, the most wonderful Person among all time's figures of fame.

2. That Person is Loved

Look now at the second special feature in our text. Not only does Christianity centre in a Person, but *that Person is loved.* The verse says, "Whom having not seen, ye love." Surely that also is a peculiar differential of Christianity.

I have seen the Mohammedans at their prayers in the magnificent Mohammed Ali Mosque at Cairo, with its alabaster walls and costly roofings of gold and silver. I have watched them in the huge Mosque of Omayad at Damascus, with its marvellous walls of fine mosaic, its exquisitely patterned ceilings and superb minarets. I have seen them in their hundreds at their preliminary ablutions and then at their regularised prostrations. I have noted their flashing-eyed zeal, their almost fierce-looking devoutness. Yet about it all there was nothing of love. Mohammed is the prophet, the champion, the teacher, to be followed and obeyed, even to the unsheathing of the sword; but he was no apostle of love, and it would be wide of the mark to say that he himself is *loved*, in the proper and tender meaning of that word.

I have wandered among the congested, unsanitary, fantastic shrines of India's sacred city, Benares, and have seen Hindus by the score showering food and petals, with pathetic credulity, on bits of scarecrow idols, only to have their oblations immediately licked off again by the tongues of observant cows. I have seen the bowing and scraping devotees in some of the most extravagant and renowned show-temples of Hinduism—the Shri Lakshminarain in New Delhi, with its florid bizarreness; the Kali Ghat Temple of Calcutta, where the stenches from dirt, drain, and disease have been nauseating. I have seen Hindu priests shooing and shoving the ill-clad crowds out of their way, glaring and glowering at those who dawdled about it; emaciated religious beggars lying along the gutter; and women even drinking water from the drain so as to please the god, and be able to bear children. Yes, we have seen it, and have turned away heart-sickened at the abject hopelessness and ugly lovelessness of it all.

Oh, how different is it when one turns to the faith and the followers of the Lord Jesus! Here is a religion of *love*; and the first aspect of that love is the love which exists between the individual believer and Christ. Away yonder, in Jos, Nigeria, I addressed a large crowd of mingling blacks and whites in a public hall, and just before I started a brother came to the platform and sang,

> "Jesus is the sweetest name I know,
>   And He's just the same
>   As His lovely name.
> That's the reason why I love Him so,
> Oh, Jesus is the sweetest name I know."

Away in the depths of the Congo jungle, it was my privilege to address over twelve hundred Christian negroes, through two interpreters; and just before I spoke, those twelve hundred sang,

with a fervour equalling that of any Christian congregation in
Britain or America,

> "My Jesus, I love Thee,
>   I know Thou art mine;
> For Thee all the pleasures
>   Of sin I resign."

In California I stood before an invited company of principals,
professors, tutors, ministers and college intellectuals; and heard
them preface my address with,

> "Jesus, the very thought of Thee
>   With sweetness fills my breast;
> But sweeter far Thy face to see,
>   And in Thy presence rest."

On a Saturday night in Australia, a crowded gathering of
exuberant city youths preluded my address by a young man's
solo, the chorus of which still haunts my inward ears—

> "Now I belong to Jesus,
>   Jesus belongs to me;
> Not for the years of time alone,
>   But for eternity!"

So it is, all round the world, where New Testament Christianity
is intelligently received: this song of love to Jesus rises daily to
heaven from millions of hearts. Jesus never marshalled an army,
never drew a sword, never used force; yet there are more people
on earth today who would gladly die for Him if needed, than there
are for any other name or cause! There is nothing like it in any
other religion, either past or present.

3. This Love is Extraordinary

Look next at the third notable feature in our text. Not only is
Jesus loved, but the love which all of us present-day Christians
bear toward Him is of an extraordinary kind. It is a love for One
whom we have never seen. The text says, "Whom *having not
seen,* ye love."

Peter himself, of course, had seen Jesus in the flesh, but the persons to whom he wrote this epistle had not. That is why he uses the pronoun "ye", and not "we": "Whom having not seen, ye love." Not one among all the millions of Christians on earth today has seen Christ in the flesh; yet in our millions we love Him with a true and heartfelt reality.

Did you ever hear of a love like that in any other connection? So far as I myself can think, it is the only case of its kind. It is arresting and unique. Did you ever hear of a young man falling in love and keeping in love with a young woman never once seen by him? Did you ever hear anywhere else of people going all through life loving someone never once seen and absolutely unseeable by them, and loving that one so dearly as to be willing even to give up life itself on that account, if need be? Is not such love extraordinary? Is there any parallel to it in any other religion, extinct or extant?

Think how much all other loves are dependent on sight and on the other physical senses. In the awakening and continuing of love between one person and another there is almost invariably an interplay of mutual physical attractiveness. There is something captivating about the face, the eyes, the lips, the features, the expression as a whole; the way of looking or smiling; the tone of voice; the winsome manner of saying or doing things. And when death takes our dear ones from us, the love which survives in our hearts for them feeds upon those characteristics which we have seen in them while they were still on earth with us.

In the case of the Christian's love for Christ it is completely otherwise. We have never once seen Him, never had even a glimpse of Him; and we have simply no reliable idea what He was like physically. We have never known one glance of His eye; never heard one tone of His voice; never felt one touch of His hand. It has been truly observed that the Gospel writers give "no hint as to Christ's personal appearance, the colour of His hair or eyes, the cast of His features, the form of His head, the fashion of His body. Christ, as to physique, is to us an absolutely unknown Being". Yet He is truly and deeply loved by a mighty multitude on earth today.

Some years ago, when we were in Cairo, we saw in an Egyptian museum a lock of hair from the head of Queen Tyi, grandmother to the wife of the now famous King Tutan-Kamun. Little did Queen Tyi dream that a lock of her hair would be on show to people like ourselves, these thousands of years later. Yet there it is, an object of curiosity among those relics of ancient Egypt.

We do not possess even a lock of hair from the head of our Lord Jesus, nor anything that He wore, nor anything that He used, despite the superstitious inventions, images, and fake-relics of the Roman Catholics. Yet in our millions, there are those of us on earth today who love Him, having never seen Him, and not knowing what He was like in feature.

But how can such a strange-seeming phenomenon really be? It is because this love for Christ is something not merely of the senses but of the spirit. It is a *spiritual* attraction and affection. Christ has appealed not merely to eye and ear, but to heart and mind. Not for a handsome face or a thrilling voice or a winning demeanour, merely, do we love Him, but for the sheer moral and spiritual and divine loveliness which is His as revealed in His teaching, in His character, and in His sublime self-sacrifice on Calvary to redeem us.

Yet while we are everlastingly grateful for what our precious Lord did for us, on the Cross, we do not stop even there. Gratitude for salvation is the first but not the final form of Christian love. We love Him, not only for what He did, but for what He *is* in Himself, as the Holy Spirit makes Him glorious to our inmost consciousness. We see Him with the eyes of the mind, not those of the body; and the love which springs therefrom transcends that of the senses.

So far as most persons are concerned, a life-like photograph or portrait of them is almost as good as a biography. As the late Dr. A. M. Fairbairn says, "How much better do we understand Dante when we study his sad yet severe, worn yet ethereal face, with its keen, clear-cut features, yet look as of infinite remoteness from the world most men realise; or Luther, when we examine the lines of his heavy and broad, yet massive and mighty countenance, so full of laughter or tears, the loud indignation of the controversialist and the inflexible resolution that could stand solitary against the world."

Yes, that may be so with others, but it is not so with Christ.

So little is flesh, face, or form capable of expressing the grace and truth of His infinitely pure and loving heart that a mere physical delineation of Him would be a very doubtful if not dangerous accessory to our faith and love, at least while we are in this present state on earth.

As dear old Dr. F. B. Meyer put it, "The great painters of Christendom covered the walls of picture galleries with conceptions of the face of Jesus. Crowds have stood transfixed and touched before those masterpieces of art. But who has not turned from the very noblest of them with a sigh of dissatisfaction, and a secret conviction that even if the sublimest feature were to be taken out of each separate picture and all combined into one, the face so composed must still fall infinitely short of that in which deity and humanity met, and shone, and wept, and loved? We shall never see anything worthy of that face till we 'see Him as He is'." "Whom *having not seen,* ye love!"

Well, there it is; this love for the unseen Christ is found in millions of human hearts today in all five continents. During recent travels I have traced it and followed it and seen it extending like a globe-girdling cord from the purple heather of Scotland, over the American Rockies and round the Blue Mountains of Australia, across the Khonds and Himalayas of India, up over Nigerian plain and plateau, on through Congo jungle-clearings, along Mediterranean coastlines, and back again to our own shores. Its degree varies in differing types of persons, and at different stages of spiritual development, but it is the same in its *nature* everywhere.

Everywhere, also, it is the same in its *effects.* It transforms sack-cloth into raiment of rejoicing. It gives beauty for ashes, the oil of joy for mourning, and the garment of praise for the spirit of heaviness. It soothes sorrows, heals wounds, and drives away fears. It makes cowards brave, and nerves feeble arms for godly exploits in the holy war of right against wrong. Wherever Christ is proclaimed and received and loved, there follows a train of gladness and singing, utterly unlike the superstitious incantations or gloomy dirges of heathen religions. As Peter says, "Whom having not seen, ye love; in Whom, though now ye see Him not, yet believing *ye rejoice with joy unspeakable and full of glory.*"

It is this love for Christ which has sent martyrs exulting to torture and flames. It is this love which keeps Christian missionaries unflaggingly toiling amid the heats and fevers and dangers and discouragements of difficult mission stations. More than anything else in the world this love to Christ purifies and dignifies and glorifies human personality. It is a love which springs from all that is highest and truest inside us toward that which is highest and sublimest outside us, even to Him who is the sum and crown of all moral excellence.

Glance again at the text: "Whom having not seen, ye love." It is true of all Christian hearts. It is true of ourselves; *but to what degree?* We love Him; but how much? Is our love for Him an expulsive power which ejects all unworthy cargo overboard? Is it an intense flame which burns away the dross of baseness and selfishness and unforgivingness, and refines our whole nature?

Let me question my own heart: Is my love for Christ a constraint strong enough to send me, if called, to "the uttermost part of the earth" as a missionary? Is it a devotion passionate enough to have me break at Christ's feet the alabaster box of all my talents and treasures for His service in the homeland? I simply cannot love Him too much. The peril, the shame, the regret is that I love Him too little. Must I not say to Him now, with fresh ardour,

> How can I, Lord, withhold
>   Life's brightest hour
> From Thee, or gathered gold,
>   Or any power?
> Why should I keep one precious thing from Thee,
> When Thou hast given Thine own dear Self for me?

If that is the present language of our hearts, what heightened bliss will be ours in the sinless rapture of that consummation yet to be when we shall *see* Him! For indeed, some golden daybreak, this unseen Christ will be seen. Faith will become perfected in sight, and love will see the Beloved's face without any intervening veil! "It doth not yet appear what we shall be; but we know that when He shall appear, we shall be like Him, for *we shall see Him as He is!*"

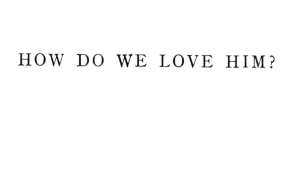

HOW DO WE LOVE HIM?

"If I really love Him, my innate and persistent selfishness will have received its death-blow."

Alexander Smellie.

He best can part with life without a sigh
Whose daily living is to daily die.

C. H. Spurgeon.

HOW DO WE LOVE HIM?

"I love my master . . . I will not go out free."—Exod. xxi. 5.

ONE of the first laws or principles in homiletics and hermeneutics is that a text must not be taken out of its context. Having stated the law, may I beg permission to break it? Somehow, as my mind lingers again over these words—"I love my master . . . I will not go out free", they assume a meaning far bigger than their local connection in Exodus xxi. The only comment I here make on the text in its context is that we must never think of the master-and-slave relationship denoted in Exodus xxi as being anything like those horrible forms of inhuman slavery exercised by white traders over the negroes in more recent centuries. An examination of the Mosaic regulations soon settles that; and I leave it there.

Let me now read the words again, in their larger, higher, Christian applicability—"I love my Master . . . I will not go out free." As soon as I thus relate the words, I myself am the grateful bondman, and the lovely Master is my Lord Jesus.

My Master

Oh, what a Master He is! How *proud* of Him I well may be! There is none like Him among all the other sons of human mothers. How poverty-stricken, by comparison, are Confucius, Buddha, Mohammed, and others whom misguided millions have fallen to worshipping! With His matchless manhood and incomparable character in view, who could seriously propose a competitor? Friends and foes alike must concur in acknowledging His solitary sinlessness and moral transcendence. I think it was Dr. Carnegie Simpson who aptly observed that if any of the renowned figures of the past—such as Confucius, Buddha, Socrates, Plato, or Shakespeare or Milton, walked in upon us, we should "take off our hats to them", whereas if Jesus came into the room we should instinctively "fall down and worship Him".

Jesus is *different*. He is an altogether unparalleled phenomenon of history. He is not complimented, nay, He is pathetically misapprehended when we think to adulate Him by calling Him even the greatest of religious philosophers or originators. He is nothing less and none other than the *GOD-MAN*, the most astounding mystery of the Deity, and the embodiment of an exquisitely perfect humanity. Truly has it been said: He came from the bosom of the heavenly Father to the bosom of an earthly mother. He took our human nature that we might partake of His divine nature. He became the Son of Man that we might become the sons of God. He was born in a cattle-shed, reared in obscurity, and lived in poverty. He had neither training nor education. Only once did He ever cross the boundary of His little native land, and even that was in babyhood. Yet His birth set angels singing, and wise men worshipping, and shepherds wondering; and even the stars sent a diamond-fingered representative to point down on His strange cradle.

In infancy He startled a king. In boyhood He puzzled the learned. In manhood He ruled even the forces of nature. He taught with an originality and authority, a simplicity and profundity, outmatching all others. He never confessed sin, and never once betrayed the slightest consciousness of it. His life and character were such that friends and foes alike were one in testifying to His moral flawlessness. He healed the multitudes without medicine and without money. He never wrote a book, yet there are more books about Him today than about any other. He never wrote a song, yet He has furnished the theme of more songs than all others combined. He never founded a college, yet all the schools together cannot boast as many students as He. He never practised medicine, yet He has healed more broken human lives than any other physician ever known. He never marshalled an army, yet no leader ever drew more volunteers ready to sacrifice everything gladly for His sake.

Great men have come and gone, yet He lives on. Herod could not kill Him in childhood. Satan could not seduce Him in manhood. Though He voluntarily laid down His life, even death could not destroy Him, and the grave could not hold Him. The past cannot confine Him. He lives in the present, the Contemporary of every generation. He is the only Being in the universe at present with an immortal human body. He is the risen, reigning, returning Lord; and His first coming as Saviour will be crowned by His second coming as Sovereign. He is the ever-living, ever-loving, everlasting Saviour who saves to the uttermost all who come unto God by Him!

That is "my Master"; and the most wonderful thing of all, so far as concerns me individually, is that this glorious Master *died for me,* as my substitutionary Sinbearer, and then *rose from the dead,* to be my ever-living Saviour. How strange if I did not love Him! Is it to be wondered at, if I love Him far more earnestly than any Israelite bondman of olden time ever loved his most generous and considerate Hebrew master? Is it to be wondered at, that all of us in our millions who know Him as our Saviour love Him as our dearest possession? Is it to be wondered at that Peter should write, "Unto you therefore which believe He is precious" (1 Pet. ii. 7)? Nay, let me avow it again: "I love my Master . . . I will not go out free."

My love to Him

This, however, opens up a big and tender question: Do all Christians love Him in the same way, or to the same degree? Let it be understood that by the word, "Christian", here, we mean only those who have actually received Christ into their hearts as a living Saviour. We are not including those many thousands of others who are only nominally Christians, who pass as Christians because they are members of churches, or because they accept Christian beliefs and morals in general. What about those of us who, by the grace of God and despite our deep unworthiness, have really been brought into saving union with Christ? Do all of us love Christ in the same way, or to the same degree? Do we all love Him as we *ought,* or as we *might?* Should we not all covet to love Him in the *deepest* way, and to the *utmost* degree?

I suppose there is a deep, underlying sense in which we all *do* love Him in the same way; for real love is always love, however varied may be the hearts in which it lives. Yet there is another sense in which no two hearts can love alike. *You* can never love Jesus just as *I* can; nor can *I* ever love Him just as *you* can. As with other things, so with love, its forms and kinds and peculiarities of expression are determined by the nature and character of the persons who love. Our Lord seeks the love of our hearts just as they are. He wants our human love just in the way which belongs to each of us individually.

Many eager-hearted disciples seem to think that in loving the Lord Jesus they must contrive to culture a kind of *religious* love, because of who He is. They try to love Him with a sombre-robed solemnity supposedly befitting His divine dignity. The motive is good, but the idea itself is mistaken. If it does not gradually smother real love, it tends to make it artificial. Would you and I have our Lord Jesus love *us* with that sort of love? Do we not glory in the thought that He loves us with all the spontaneous compassion and affection and delight of His great heart?

When our Lord restored fallen Peter, as recorded in John xxi, He asked him three times, "Simon, son of Jonas, lovest thou Me?" When Peter replied, "Yea, Lord, Thou knowest that I love thee", the Greek word which he used for "love" was different from that which our Lord had used in His question. Peter used the verb, *philo*, which denotes purely human affection; and he kept to it in each of his three replies. To my own mind, one of the most significant features in the incident is that our Lord *accepted* Peter's word as the basis for a new commission to service and leadership. To love our Lord reverently does not mean that I must love Him unnaturally, solemnly, "religiously". On the contrary, He wants me to love Him in just the way that *my* poor heart loves. He wants all the eager, spontaneous, affectionate response to Him of which my heart is capable, just as it is.

> Yes, I may love Thee, dearest Lord,
>   All-glorious as Thou art;
> For Thou hast stooped to ask of me
>   The love of my poor heart.

The more we thus love Him, naturally, hungrily, eagerly, reverently, devotedly, practically, so the more does this loving purify the heart, and refine the mind, and increase our *capacity* to love him. So, also, does it increase our capacity to enjoy *His* love toward *us*.

But, of course, our love to Christ may assume various forms or features of outreach; and these we should clearly distinguish, as follows.

Ways and Degrees of Loving Him

Often our minds can best lay hold of a subject by breaking it up into its several parts or aspects. It may be helpful, therefore, if we distinguish the *ways* in which we may love Him. I think it is true, in general, that the *way* in which we love Him determines the *degree* to which we love Him.

Gratefully.

We usually begin by loving our Lord *gratefully*. When at our conversion we receive Him as Saviour, our minds are filled with thankful wonder at what He has *done* for us. In most cases there has been a prelude of "conviction". The Holy Spirit has made us to know our sinfulness and exposure to eternal ruin; He has disturbed the conscience, and awakened us to the terrors of coming judgment; He has also made Christ real to us as our substitutionary Sinbearer and Saviour. And now, as with dread concern and repentant heart we see Christ bleeding on the Cross to redeem us, how wonderful He becomes! Oh, that He should thus suffer for our sakes! Oh, that He should so willingly yield His back to the scourge and His face to the smiters! Oh, that He should voluntarily and vicariously undergo that depthless agony on our behalf! Truly, "His name shall be called Wonderful"!

From then our response to Him begins to express itself in exclamations of upsurging gratitude. Nothing more fittingly voices our feelings than the little chorus,

> Oh, the love that sought me !
> Oh, the blood that bought me !
> Oh, the grace that brought me
>   to the fold !

In the words of 1 John iv. 19, "We love Him *because He first loved us*." Our love is that of *gratitude*. Our marvelling articulates itself in such words as Paul's, "The Son of God loved *me*, and gave Himself for *me*" (Gal. ii. 20). Verses like 2 Corinthians viii. 9, light up with such almost unbelievable glory of meaning that we cannot think why they never overpowered us before— "Ye know the grace of our Lord Jesus Christ, that though He was rich, yet for our sakes He became poor, that we through His poverty might become rich."

Of course, this loving Christ *gratefully* goes on and on in the Christian life, becoming ever truer and deeper as our mental apprehension of the Cross enlarges. The more discerningly we penetrate the profound meaning and vast woe of that redeeming sacrifice, the more does our gratitude abound, so that the older believer even more than the younger is "lost in wonder, love, and praise".

Notwithstanding this, however, I think it true that this loving Christ *gratefully* is the most characteristic mark of the new convert. Some time ago I was hearing of a workman who fell into the water at Woolwich docks, London. He could scarcely swim, and over against the weight of his heavy shoes and clothes in the oily waters he just had no chance. But the under-manager of a nearby shipping office saw what had happened, tore off his overcoat and shoes, and dived to the rescue. After a struggle he got the exhausted workman to a place where they were both hauled up to safety. Two mornings later, the under-manager was told that a woman wished to see him. She brought three young children with her, and this is what she said: "Excuse me, sir, but are you the gentleman that saved my Jim? Oh, pardon me for comin' in, sir, but me and the children just couldn't help it. Jim's such a lovin' husband and father. You'll never know, sir, what you've done for us, nor how much we thanks you." By this time tears were dripping down her bonny face; and then she added, "We've no money to pay a reward, sir, but would you mind, sir, . . . would you mind if me and the children kissed you?" Perhaps the under-manager began to feel that *he* now needed to be rescued! But can we not enter into the woman's feelings? She knew nothing about the under-manager except this, that he had saved her precious husband; but that was enough to make him wonderful, and to move her with deep gratitude.

Even so, when we first come to know Christ, our minds are mainly captivated by what He has *done* for us. What is any merely physical rescue compared with the spiritual and eternal deliverance which *He* has effected for *us*? Has He not delivered us from "the power of darkness" and translated us into His own kingdom? Has He not forever saved us from "the outer darkness" and the flame of Gehenna? Has He not made us "partakers in the inheritance of the saints in light"? Has He not made us "sons of God" and "joint heirs" with Himself to eternal glories? Can we, or dare we even try to subdue our irrepressible testimony? —

> He found me with a burden,
>   And He lifted it from me;
> He found me bound and fettered,
>   And from sin He set me free.
> He found me in the darkness,
>   And He made His light to shine.
> Can you wonder that I love Him,
>   This Saviour-Friend divine?

This Christward love which springs from *gratitude* may be the earliest and most elementary form of our love to Him, yet when it powerfully takes hold of the mind, and especially when it becomes infused by deeper kinds of love, it mightily affects the whole life. One of the most greatly used and widely known of Christian missionaries left on record that the mainspring of his life and labours had been this: "If Jesus Christ died that Calvary death for me, then no sacrifice can ever be too great that I can make for Him." Motivated by the same gratitude, the youthful David Livingstone wrote: "I will place no value on anything I have or may possess, except in relation to the kingdom of Christ." When the Moravian missionary, Dober, went out to the black people at St. Thomas, and was told that he would never reach the slaves because he was not a slave himself, he actually sold himself into slavery to get among them and tell them of the Saviour. There was an African girl, too, who sold herself into slavery that the price of her market-value might be used to send the Gospel of Christ to others of her tribe. But we must stay our hand! We are starting something here which would require a volume all to itself, were we to continue. "The time would fail to tell" of the many thousands who in grateful love to Christ have gladly sacrificed for His dear sake. Did not our Lord Himself once tell us that they who are forgiven much love much (Luke vii. 47)? Two thousand years have shown how true that is. Those who have most deeply realised how great is the eternal ruin from which they have been rescued, and how great is the love which suffered to save them, have gladly exclaimed, as the willing slaves of Jesus, "I love my Master; *I will not go out free.*"

Reciprocally.

So, then, we start by loving Christ gratefully; but as we make progress in the Christian life we learn to love Him *reciprocally*. He has not only done something inexpressibly wonderful *for* us; He has come to us invisibly yet none-the-less personally to *indwell* us, and to share our life with us. He promised to do this when we received Him as our Saviour. "Behold, I stand at the door, and knock. If any man hear My voice, and open the door, I will come in to him, *and will sup with him, and he with Me*" (Rev. iii. 20).

After conversion, this mutual sharing and reciprocal feasting gradually become a gladsome reality in the experience of the earnest believer. Many of us who have now known the Saviour for twenty or thirty or forty years or more, can vividly recall those early espousals of our love to Him; those first seasons of secret communion with Him; those first mountain-top moments when He appeared to our inward eyes as we meditated in His Word; those occasions of solemn rapture during our young discipleship when we suddenly, almost stunningly *realised* His presence with us, watching, listening, understanding, caring, loving. Oh, it was all so unspeakable to our newly-regenerated hearts. I can remember how truly at that time the words of a favourite hymn became my own language:

> Jesus, these eyes have never seen
>   That radiant form of Thine;
> The veil of sense hangs dark between
>   Thy blessed face and mine.

> I see Thee not, I hear Thee not,
>   Yet Thou art oft with me;
> And earth hath ne'er so dear a spot
>   As where I meet with Thee.

As the months and years slip away, Jesus becomes a firmer and fonder fact in the experience of the responsive, prayerful believer. Even the deepest *self*-consciousness gradually becomes interpenetrated by a sublimating *Christ*-consciousness. It begins to be a strange wonder how other people can live without Him. He becomes indispensable to heart and mind. He shares every experience, transforming and enriching all by His sympathetic participation and constancy. When the stormy blast beats about us, He is always there to enwrap us in the mantle of His mighty care. When the battle rages fierce and hot, He is ever in the thick of it with us to defend us. When the bitter grapes of sorrow are wrung out to us, none can sweeten our cup as He. He is our "refuge" in every emergency; and our "strength" in every encounter with evil; and our "very present help" in every trouble.

Thus there evolves a reciprocal companionship between the believer and the Lord. There is a mutual sharing going on all the time. The Christian heart learns ever-increasingly to love Him, not only gratefully as the One who has wrought a stupendous rescue, but as the unseen yet ever-present and indwelling Friend who "knows all about our struggles" and who "guides till the day is done". There develops a love-bond like that between Jonathan and David, or like that between Ruth and Naomi, only far more sacred and spiritual. We love Him now, not only "because He first loved us" (1 John iv. 19), but because He has become the "Friend which sticketh closer than a brother" (Prov. xviii. 24); not only because of what He has *done* for us, but because of what He has *become* to us. We prove Him experientially day by day, and learn to love Him in return for all that He now means to us. That is, we love Him *reciprocally*; our experience is that of the hymn which says,

> He is not a disappointment,
>   He is all-in-all to me;
> Saviour, Sanctifier, Healer,
>   The unchanging Friend is He.
> He has *won my heart's affection*,
>   For He *meets my every need*.
> He is not a disappointment,
>   For He satisfies indeed.

Adoringly.

But it is time we came to deeper depths. Besides loving Christ gratefully and reciprocally, there is a loving Him *adoringly*. By this we mean loving Him, not merely because of what He has done for us, or because of what He now means to us, but because of *what He is in Himself*. Pure love is the noblest outreach of which the human heart is capable; and Christ is the most transcendently loveable Object upon which it can spend itself. In Him are sheer infinitudes of perfect moral excellence and beauty. He is indeed "the chiefest among ten thousand", and the "altogether lovely" (Song v. 10, 16). As we prayerfully familiarise ourselves with the Lord Jesus Christ of the Gospels and the Epistles, it is not long before we are at His feet, exclaiming with Thomas, "My Lord, and my God!" It is not long before we find ourselves, with apostle John, beholding in Him "the glory as of the Only-begotten of the Father, full of grace and truth".

On earth He lived the most strangely and compellingly beautiful life ever seen or known. He was the purest, noblest, strongest, tenderest, loftiest, humblest, kindliest, most patient, sympathetic, utterly virtuous character ever clothed with human nature. His self-abnegating otherism was sublime. So intent was He on relieving others that He forgot food for Himself. It was His very breath to share, to soothe, to help, to forgive, and to love with a great-hearted compassion. He never answered, Nay, when a needy one sought His aid, nor turned away when request for help in trouble was made. He so lived that He willingly died for those who least deserved it, and with no retaliation except to pray, "Father, forgive them; they know not what they do." The utter meekness and sinless simplicity of His life are only equalled by the sheer majesty and glory of it. Of Him alone could it be even hyperbolically written that if all His deeds of kindness should be recorded, "even the world itself could not contain the books that should be written".

Oh, what an ineffable Object of adoration Jesus is. Turn to the hymn-book again, and let some of the rapturous expressions of adoration there tell us what Christ means to the contemplation of the consecrated soul.

Take the famous missionary Hudson Taylor's favourite hymn, written by Jean Sophie Pigott:

> Jesus I am resting, resting
>   In the joy of *what Thou art*.
> I am finding out the greatness
>   Of Thy loving heart.
> Thou hast bid me gaze upon Thee,
>   And *Thy beauty fills my soul*,
> For by Thy transforming power
>   Thou hast made me whole.

See how the saintly Bernard of Clairvaux's yearning delight in Christ breathes itself through his oft-sung lines:

> Jesus the very thought of Thee
>   With sweetness fills my breast;
> But sweeter far Thy face to see,
>   And in Thy presence rest.

Turn to the eloquent F. W. Faber, and see in some of his lines what one can only describe as a burning ardour of adoration:

> O Jesus! Jesus! dearest Lord,
>   Thy sacred name I say
> For very love within my heart
>   Unnumbered times a day.
>
> I love Thee so, I know not how
>   My rapture to control;
> Thy love is like a burning fire
>   Within my very soul.
>
> For Thou to me art all in all,
>   My honour and my wealth,
> My heart's desire, my daily strength,
>   My soul's eternal health.
>
> Burn, burn, O Love, within my heart,
>   Burn ceaseless, night and day,
> Till all unworthy other loves
>   Are wholly burned away.

And here is Antoinette Bourignon's hymn, which in my boyhood days used to be sung in our Methodist Class Meetings by shining-faced lovers of the Lord:

> Come, Saviour, Jesus, from above!
>   Assist me with Thy heavenly grace:
> Empty my heart of earthly love,
>   And for Thyself prepare the place.
>
> Thee I can love, and Thee alone,
>   With pure delight and inward bliss:
> To know Thou makest me Thine own,
>   What utter happiness is this!
>
> Henceforth may no profane delight
>   Divide this consecrated soul;
> Possess it Thou, who hast the right,
>   As Lord and Master of the whole.

And here are some verses from a more recent collection speaking this same fervent language of enraptured adoration:

> Saviour, I love and adore Thee:
> Joy of all joys—Thou art mine!
> Whom should I treasure before Thee?
> Where is such beauty as Thine?
> How could I ever but love Thee?
> Who can with Thee compare?
> Who in all heav'n is above Thee
> Who on the earth is so fair?

> .   .   .   .   .

> No angel's tongue above
> Could e'er express His love;
> Nor harp of sweetest sound
> Like His dear voice be found.
> No lustrous seraph there
> Could e'er with Him compare—
> The fairest of the fair
> is Jesus.

> .   .   .   .   .

> No gem in earth or sea
> Could be so dear as He,
> Nor ought in heav'n to me
> like Jesus.

We are reminded of the dear old Puritan preacher who in a fervour of anticipation exclaimed, "When I get to heaven, I shall spend the first thousand years looking at JESUS; and then I may have a look round!" We are reminded, too, of Lydia Muller, daughter of the saintly and famous George Muller, founder of the Bristol Orphan Homes. Soon after her spirit had slipped away from the tired and poorly body, there was found by her bedside a verse which she had written shortly before:

> I have seen the face of Jesus;
> Tell me not of ought beside.
> I have heard the voice of Jesus;
> All my soul is satisfied.

The very highest attraction of heaven to all such lovers of Christ is that of consummated adoration and possession of *HIM*. We think of Mrs. Cousins and her well-known lines:

The Lamb there in His beauty
Without a veil is seen;
It were a well-spent journey
Though seven deaths lay between.

If we turn from the hymn-book to some of the writings of those who have known Jesus best, what testimonies in prose we find concerning His matchless appeal! Let Samuel Rutherford tell us. He says: "Every day we see some new thing in Christ. His love hath neither brim nor bottom. This soul of ours hath love, and cannot but love some fair one; and oh, what a fair One, what an only One, what an excellent, lovely, ravishing One is Jesus!"

John Fawcett, writer of the well-worn hymn, "Blest be the tie that binds . . ." once wrote a little book, *Christ Precious*. When I was a young Christian I used to carry it in my pocket, and read it on long, lonely walks over Lancashire's Pennine hills. Sometimes I could scarcely read it for tears of joy that such a Saviour was mine. I have long since lost that rich little pocket companion, but here is just one little extract from it which I jotted down to quote in one of the earliest public addresses which I ever dared to preach: "O blessed Jesus, Thy love is wonderful. The experiential sense of it here on earth sweetens the bitterness of life and disarms death of all its terrors. Thou art the full ocean of never-failing delight and satisfaction. When I am favoured with the sense of Thy love, my soul is filled and satisfied."

We could fill a book with such quotations, but must forbear! Those which we have here culled, almost at random, from verse and prose, are simply a specimen "cluster of the grapes" from Eshcol, representing the glorious, endless vintage of this rich Canaan.

Oh, that you and I may be so taken up with our dear Lord that we love Him in like fashion! In these days we are cursed by a restless hurry which unfits the mind for long-lingering meditation and communion. Many people think they are cramming more into their life by what they call "our wonderful modern speed", when what they are really doing is crowding out those things which most enrich life! We need not envy the restless speeders; we may rather pity them. This is the age of science, invention, mechanics, automaticity, swift mobility—and *superficiality*. Our Lord calls His people away from the merciless, non-stop whirl of the outer world, to quiet, secret, unhurried trysting with Himself. He has lovely secrets to tell those who wait long enough. He still "manifests" Himself to those who love Him enough to tarry long and often in His presence. He is still the One in whom are hid all those imperishable treasures for which the human heart fundamentally craves. Oh, to wait before Him till we really *see* Him with the eyes of the soul! Oh, to seek Him until we really *find* Him as heaven itself come down into our hearts!

> But what to those who find? Ah, this;
> Nor tongue, nor pen can show:
> The love of Jesus, what it is,
> None but His loved ones know.

Absorbingly.

So, then, we may love Christ gratefully, reciprocally, adoringly, yet we cannot end even at adoration. There is a further reach. There is a breadth and length and depth and height which we can only describe as loving Christ *absorbingly*. Adoration is a worshipful contemplation of Christ, and a complacent delight in Him; but it is not active appropriation or absorption. There is a love which, however much it adores, cannot rest there; it must claim; it must embrace; it must possess. Nay, the more devoutly it adores, the more pained it becomes to reach and hold and become united in one with that which it loves. This kind of love says to Christ,

> I cannot breathe enough of Thee,
> Thou gentle breath of love.
> More fragrant than the myrtle tree,
> The rose of Sharon is to me,
> The balm of heaven above.

There is a love for Christ which is such a pure white flame of spiritual desire toward Him that it begets a kind of holy love-sickness if it is not continually satisfied by rich, deep, absorbing communion with Him. Take that well-known verse of Charles Wesley's,

> Oh, love divine, how sweet Thou art!
> When shall I find my willing heart
> All taken up by Thee?
> I thirst, I faint, I die, to prove
> The fulness of redeeming love,
> Thy love, O Christ, to me.

See the increasing longing expressed in that fourth line—"I *thirst*", and then, "I *faint*", and then even, "I *die*". We are beyond the depth of many Christian believers now. They wade in shallower waters. To use Ezekiel's phraseology, there are those who are in waters "to the ankles"; and there are those who are in waters "to the knees"; and there are those who are in waters "to the loins"; but in Charles Wesley's stanza we have reached the "waters to swim in" (Ezek. xlvii. 3–5). We have reached the point where the soul says to Christ, in the words of David, "Thy love to me is wonderful, passing the love of women" (2 Sam. i. 26). We have tasted the pure bliss which His Self-communicating fellowship imparts to the consecrated heart. All other things pale into comparative nothingness. We must now have *HIM,* or life is not life at all. We say with David, "Thy lovingkindness is better than life" . . . "My soul followeth hard after Thee" (Ps. lxiii. 3, 8). We "sit down under His shadow with great delight, and His fruit is sweet to our taste" (Song ii. 3). He has become our all-in-all. We simply cannot do without Him. We find ourselves saying to Him, "Life is dark without Thee. Death with Thee is bright." He becomes nothing less than

> My God, the spring of all my joys,
>   The life of my delights;
> The glory of my brightest days,
>   The comfort of my nights!

> In darkest shades, if Thou appear,
>   My dawning is begun;
> Thou art my soul's bright morning star,
>   And Thou my rising sun!

When the soul loves Christ after this fashion, times of prayer are raptures of communion. Again and again we break into exclamations like that of dear old William Carvosso, one of the early Methodists of Cornwall—"Oh, the inexpressible blessedness arising from a heartfelt union with the Son of God!" We say with the hymn-verse,

> Nothing on earth do I desire
>   But Thy pure love within my breast.
> This, only this, do I require,
>   And freely give up all the rest!

Our longing is that of Shulamith toward her royal bridegroom, "Let me hear Thy voice; for sweet is Thy voice, and Thy countenance is comely." The quintessence of our joy is to know and say, "My beloved is mine, and I am His." Moreover, our longing is *satisfied,* for to the soul which is now completely His of its own free choice and by unreserved self-surrender, our Lord "manifests" Himself in a way which is impossible to others. Oh, when we know and possess and enjoy Him thus, then we know the rapture of satisfied soul-hunger in Faber's words,

> Oh, light in darkness! joy in grief!
> Oh, wealth beyond all worth!
> Jesus! my Love! To have Thee mine
> Is *heaven begun on earth*

How many, or how few of us, I wonder, love and possess our Lord in *this* way? It is a glorious thing to be His at all—to be saved; to know Him; to trust and love Him. Praised be He for all those who have learned to love Him gratefully, reciprocally, adoringly. But should not you and I covet to be in that inner circle of those who love Him *absorbingly*? Truly, there is a love for Christ of such a kind and degree that it loves its very heart away to Him, yet in losing itself finds its ecstatic fulfilment in Him. In giving itself completely to Him it lives on Him, feeds on Him, absorbs *His* love in return. We will add no more, lest with multiplicity of words we should becloud that which we are trying to clarify. There is a price to pay. There must be a saying "No" to the flesh; a conquering of prayerlessness; a putting right of wrong things in our life; a living to the honour of our Lord; and a godly determination to give *priority* to our daily seasons of secret tarrying with Him. We should unhurriedly talk over with Him the truths and promises of His written word, asking Him to fulfil them in our experience. We should discuss with Him all the details of our life, along with all the larger concerns. We should share all our secrets—everything—with Him. We should also silently contemplate and meditate upon His love, His purity, His grace, His goodness, His kindness, toward us, letting our hearts really go out to Him. As we thus "seek", we shall surely "find", to our heart's delight. Our marvel will be that for so long we denied ourselves the foretaste of heaven which comes with the deeper experience of His wonderful love.

WHAT IS MY ANSWER?

"God is very patient. It took Him years to teach me to say two words: 'Lord, anything!'"

A. Douglas Brown.

"If Jesus Christ be God, and died for me, then no sacrifice can be too great for me to make for Him."

C. T. Studd.

WHAT IS MY ANSWER?

"Lovest thou Me?"—John xxi. 15, 16, 17.

THIS is always the prime concern of Jesus with each of His disciples: "Lovest thou Me?" Here, in John xxi, the question is asked of Simon Peter; but just as truly our heavenly Master asks it of Andrew and Philip, of Thomas and Matthew, and of all His disciples from then until now. This very moment, it is His most searching question to you and me. What is our answer? Perhaps we may find help, in relating ourselves afresh to it, if we reconsider it in this early-morning setting of John xxi. 15–17:

"So when they had dined, Jesus saith to Simon Peter: Simon, son of Jonas, lovest thou Me more than these? He saith unto Him: Yea, Lord, Thou knowest that I love Thee. He saith unto him: Feed my lambs.

"He saith to him again the second time: Simon, son of Jonas, lovest thou Me? He saith unto Him: Yea, Lord, Thou knowest that I love Thee. He saith unto him: Feed my sheep.

"He saith unto him the third time: Simon, son of Jonas, lovest thou Me? Peter was grieved because He said unto him the third time, Lovest thou Me? And he said unto Him: Lord, Thou knowest all things; Thou knowest that I love Thee. Jesus saith unto him: Feed my sheep."

So "Peter was grieved" because Jesus asked him the same question three times. Afterward, however, he would be just as grateful as he was at first grieved, for he would perceive what a gracious invention of considerate love it was. How could he help but realise, soon afterward, that over against his *three cowardly denials* of Jesus on the dark betrayal night, his Lord had now gently pressed him into *three re-avowals of his love*? Without even mentioning the threefold lapse, our Lord had skilfully contrived a threefold restoration and recommissioning of His fallen apostle.

The incident is precious as indicating how our Lord deals with ourselves, when *we* have failed or fallen. Three times the Lord questions. Three times Simon replies. Three times the Lord recommissions. Thus, the interchange runs in three trios. Unfortunately, our English translation does not bring out the incidental variations of wording in the Greek. It is well worth while, therefore, to glance through the incident again, noting these changes in the three successive alternations.

The First Interchange.

Take the first of them. Our Lord asks: "Simon, son of Jonas, lovest thou Me more than these?" The Greek word for "love" here is the verb-form of *agapē*, which means love in the more elevated and spiritual sense. It is the word which is always used when *God's* love is spoken of, and which Paul uses all the way through I Corinthians xiii, his classic passage on love.

When Peter replies, however, he uses a different word for love, namely *filios*, which, although it certainly connotes love, is a less exalted word conveying fond natural affection, but nothing higher. Peter feels he has fallen so far short of the noble love which Jesus had expected and deserved from him, that he dare not use the higher word, though he can still sincerely use the other. This cautiousness indicates a changed Peter; a saddened disillusioned Peter subdued by the shattering discovery of how weak he really was when put to the test. He had once said to Jesus, "Though all men shall be offended because of Thee, yet will *I* never be offended" (Matt. xxvi. 33). He had gone even further, when he exclaimed, "Lord, why cannot I follow Thee now? I will lay down my life for Thy sake" (John. xiii. 37). These hasty avowals had cast a reflection upon the other disciples, tacitly assuming that Peter's devotion to Jesus was stronger than theirs. But now Jesus asks him, "Simon, son of Jonas, lovest thou Me *more than these do?*"—and a chastened Peter can only droop his head as he replies, "Yea, Lord, Thou knowest that (despite everything) I have true affection for Thee." He drops all comparisons with others. He knows that his very heart is being read, and he would have the great Searcher of hearts simply see his affection just as it is in itself, however much the past may have called it in question.

To this our Lord responds with, "Feed my lambs." The young

ones of the flock need special care; and our Lord's gracious implication is that if Peter has this true, natural affection for Him, then even though he will not risk avowing *more* than that, it is enough to qualify him for this tender service.

The Second Interchange.

Our Lord now asks the second time: "Simon, son of Jonas, lovest thou Me?" This time He leaves off the words, "more than these", for Peter's first reply has sufficiently indicated the collapse of his former boastfulness. But our Lord retains the higher word for love, i.e. *agapē*. In effect, this further question is, "Even though you are no longer prepared to say that you love Me more than the other disciples do, are you able to say that you love Me in that higher, more spiritual way?"

Peter's reply to *this* is a verbatim repetition of his *first* reply: "Yea, Lord, Thou knowest that I love Thee." He still uses the word for love which he used before, and does not risk using the word which Jesus used. But so long as he keeps to his own word he can say with utterly genuine affection quivering in his tones, *"Thou knowest* that I love Thee."

This brings the further word of recommission: "Feed my sheep." The first time it was "Feed my lambs"—the young and inexperienced in the Good Shepherd's Flock; but now Peter is given ministry to the full-grown sheep. It is unfortunate that our Authorised Version uses the word "Feed" again here, for a different Greek word is used which means something like our word *"tend"*.

The Third Interchange.

Finally, our Lord asks Peter the third time: "Simon, son of Jonas, lovest thou Me?" But this time He changes His word for love, and uses that which Peter had used. It was as though He said, "Even using your own word, Simon, do you really have this true affection for Me?"

We are told that "Peter was grieved because He said unto him the third time, Lovest thou Me?" But it was not merely the fact that it was the *third* asking which so hurt Peter's feelings; it was our Lord's coming down to Peter's own word, and apparently doubting whether Peter loved Him even on *that* level.

What will Peter *now* reply? Never did a human heart more frankly and appealingly lay itself bare before the omniscient Psychologist than Peter now does as he says, "Lord, Thou *knowest all things*; Thou knowest that I love Thee."

I rather think that as Peter gave this reply he lifted up his drooping head, and with reverent, appealing eyes looked right into the wonderful eyes of Jesus; and I also feel sure that as our Lord now uttered His third word of restoration, His compassionate reply-look would mean even more to Peter than the actual words—"Feed my sheep." Note that this third word of reinstatement completes a full recommissioning of Peter. First, he was to "feed" the "lambs". Secondly, he was merely to "tend" or render assistance to the "sheep". But now, third, our Lord goes all the way and says, "Feed my sheep."

It is good to get into our minds a photographic picture of this threefold interchange between our Lord and Peter, seeing the progress marked in its three stages by the changes in wording which are not shown in our English version. We need to see it mentally in three columns: in the first column our Lord's three askings; in the second column Peter's three responses; in the third column our Lord's three reinstatements; thus—

Question	Reply	Recommission
(1) "Simon, son of Jonas, *lovest* thou Me *more than these?*"	(1) "Yea, Lord, Thou knowest that I have true *affection* for Thee."	(1) "He saith unto him: Feed my *lambs*."
(2) "Simon, son of Jonas, *lovest* thou Me?"	(2) "Yea, Lord, Thou knowest that I have true *affection* for Thee."	(2) "He saith unto him: *Tend* my *sheep*."
(3) "Simon, son of Jonas, hast thou even this *affection* for Me?"	(3) "Lord, Thou knowest all things; Thou knowest I have this true *affection* for Thee."	(3) "Jesus saith unto him: *Feed* my *sheep*."

Let us now briefly review the incident in total, and then apply it to ourselves. In the first place we should appreciate the "why and wherefore" of its *necessity*. Our Lord's reiterated interlocution did not in reality imply doubt as to the sincerity of Peter's replies, but it *did* intend Peter and the other disciples to learn that the threefold denial must be expunged by a sincere threefold re-avowal, after repentance, and in the presence of other disciples. Without this, the impression might have been created that the sad lapse could be overlooked as trivial.

Next, let us gratefully appreciate the sympathetic *indirectness* of our Lord's method with Peter. Not once did He refer to the three base denials. His allusion was so veiled that it only became unmistakably detectable when for the third time He asked His question. Without even slightly mitigating the seriousness of Peter's cowardly default, He made it radiantly clear that if Peter did indeed truly love Him, then that love of his cancelled out all those ugly things of which he was now ashamed. Christian believer, ponder that well, for its implications are highly consoling. I have known Christian believers gradually lose all joy in the prospect of our Lord's second coming, because of fallings and failings in their lives which they have felt sure He would angrily expose and rebuke on His return. Oh no! Not one sincere disciple need ever have such a fear. Would ever our Lord Himself look forward joyfully to that golden hour if He were coming with thunder on His brow and stinging reprimands on His lips? Let us never cruelly wrong Him by entertaining such thoughts. If we *sincerely love* Him, there will be no mention of those other things. Is He not "touched with the feeling of our infirmities" (Heb. iv. 15)? Did He not say that even a "cup of cold water" given in His name should not lose its reward (Mark ix. 41)? And is not His treament of Peter the divinest of all commentaries on Proverbs x. 12, "Love covereth all sins"?

Again, let us see in this restoration of Peter a most heartening *encouragement* to those who have dishonoured the Name or wounded the heart of Jesus since they were converted to Him. Few of us have more ignobly denied or defamed Him than did Peter on that tragic night of long ago. Yet Peter was not only forgiven his disloyalty, but was fully restored to fellowship with his Lord, and fully recommissioned for leadership in service. And can it be that these words of mine come to some *other* remorseful, self-condemned Peter? Oh, come back to Jesus at once, with Simon's avowal on your lips—"Lord, Thou knowest all things, Thou knowest that I love Thee." He waits to be gracious. His heart melts with compassion. He has a thorough understanding of all that you now regret; and as the dear old hymn says,

> Love only waits to forgive and forget.

Just once more, we ought to underline the main *emphasis* in Peter's restoration. Our Lord puts the emphasis on love. He did not ask, "Are you sorry?" He did not ask, "Do you promise?" He did not ask, "Will you try to make amends?" No; His big concern was, "Do you *love* Me?" So has it been always, from that day to this. So is it even now, this moment; His supreme question to you and me is, "Do you *love* Me?" He can be satisfied with nothing less than that, for all in one He is our Friend, Brother, Saviour, Lord and God! Well may many of us say,

> Lord, it is my chief complaint
> That my love is weak and faint;
> Yet I love Thee, and adore;
> Oh, for grace to love Thee more!

Perhaps the most significant thing of all, however, in Peter's restoration, is that when our Lord asked Him for the third time, "Lovest thou Me?" He changed over from that higher word which He had used for love and came down to that which Peter had used—the word expressing Peter's sincere, fond, natural love for Him. Observe the precious fact carefully: Jesus accepted *that* as the satisfactory basis of restoration and new commission. So is it with all of us. He must have our love. He must come *first* in our love. But he accepts us just as we are, and our love just as it is, if we are sincere. The *other* kind of love—that higher, more spiritual and elevated love, comes in afterward, through the refining influence of the Holy Spirit, and *sublimates* our natural affection; but first and foremost our Master Jesus wants the warm, eager, spontaneous, natural love of our hearts. All too many of us fall into the mistake of thinking that when it comes to loving Jesus we must somehow work up a kind of *religious* love for Him. No!—emphatically, No! It is just *my own* love, loving Him in *its own way* that He would win; for it somehow means something to Him which the love of no other intelligence in the universe means in just the same way.

The love of my poor heart can mean,
    To God's beloved Son,
Something He nowhere else has seen,
    And in no other won.
And His dear love can be to me
    My own, my very own;
Something that He can only be
    To me, and me alone.

What Then of Ourselves?

Let us now apply the incident to our own hearts. This dear Master of ours comes to us and challenges us with the direct question, *"Lovest thou Me?"* Our answer to that question means more to Him than anything else in our relationship toward Him. It means more than giving Him our money, or using for Him our time, or rendering to Him much service, or being faithful in regular worship. He does not ask, "Do you admire Me?" or "Do you honour Me?" or "Do you worship Me?" or "Do you bear witness for Me?" or "Do you try to live according to my teachings?" He does not ask, as His first and decisive question, "Have you wept sufficiently over your failures, lapses, denials?" or "Have you fasted, made amends, tried to atone?" No; His first question *always*, and at *this very moment*, is, "Do you *love* Me?" Until we can say from a truly contrite, grateful, eager, longing heart toward Him, "Yea, Lord, Thou *knowest* that I *love* Thee", He cannot be fully satisfied toward us.

Nor is this to be wondered at. Reflect how *He* loves each of *us*. Can such love as that be content with anything *less* than love in return? Can the loving mother or father be content with mere respect or obedience in the household? Is it not the children's *love* which alone brings full reward? Can the loving bride or bridegroom find repose in anything less than *love* from the heart of the loved one? How well I remember a handsome, manly, but unhappy husband who once confided to me his distress about his charming but vain and philandering wife. "She is all I could ever wish for, in lovely looks and congenial temperament and domestic capability," he said; "and I almost worship the ground she treads on. But all these things only make it unbearably worse to endure the fact that she seems to have no real *love* for me." Is there *any* pain worse than that of deep, pure, but unrequited love?

Perhaps all such human comparisons lose some degree of relevance when we use them to illustrate the *divine* love toward us. Yet we do well to remember that in our Lord Jesus Christ, the love of God now comes to us through a human heart, and feels after us with human qualities and emotions as well as divine. I think that at present we scarcely have the slightest conception of the tenderness with which our Lord Jesus loves us; and I am certain that nothing can satisfy Him but the real, warm, deep, eager, reverent *love* of our hearts in return.

> My utter love, nor more, nor less,
>   His royal heart demands;
> My King of Love, all loveliness,
>   With nail-scars in His hands.
> And dare I love Him but in part?
>   How can I but adore,
> And love away my very heart
>   To Him for evermore?

Yes, that is what He asks of me. Nor can He ask less; for, let me remember, He is not only my truest human Friend, my only Saviour from eternal ruin, and the One who loves me more than all the others, but in Himself He is utter worth and sheer excellence; the Lord of the universe, co-equal with the Father and the Spirit in the divine Trinity who gave me my being. No, He cannot ask less; and how can I *offer* less to such an One as He?

But this leads to further considerations. If this matter of my love means so much to *Him*, it means even more to *me*. It is the determining factor in three most important issues, i.e. in my experience of sanctification; in my Christian service; and in my heavenly future.

If we think carefully, it does not take us long to see that our love to Christ is the basic factor in the blessing of *sanctification*. In my time, I have come across this and that and the other theory of holiness. There are the eradicationists, and the counteractionists, and the suppressionists; the Wesley-ites, the Holiness-School-ites, with other well-meaning "ists" and "ites". We have learned something from each and all; but when the last theoretic word has been spoken, it still remains true that the spiritual protoplasm from which all true experience of sanctification develops is our love to Christ.

We have met Christian believers who were so obsessed by some particular "doctrine" of sanctification that instead of being drawn closer to Christ and made more like Him in practical, unselfish helpfulness toward others, they have been surreptitiously lured *away* from Him into a kind of cliquish, self-deluded spiritual "superiority". On the other hand, we have met simple-hearted believers who have never once been to a "holiness" meeting, nor ever been "enlightened" by exegetical theories or interpretations of "Scriptural sanctification", who nevertheless have been right "into the blessing", rejoicing in radiant fellowship with Christ, enjoying the "overcoming life", mounting up "with wings as eagles" into "heavenly places in Christ", experiencing daily enduement with "power from on high", and living Christ-communicative lives, all because they just loved our Lord so eagerly that they could say with fine old General Booth of the Salvation Army, "Jesus has every bit of me."

When we earnestly *love* Him, do we knowingly allow in our lives anything which would dishonour His name or grieve His heart? When we earnestly *love* Him, whatever things we may want for ourselves, do we really want them at all unless it pleases Him? When we earnestly *love* Him, do we not delight in the place of secret communion with Him? When we earnestly *love* Him, do we not prize His written word as "great spoil"? Do we not pray with truer understanding that the experience of sanctification or set-apart-ness may be ours for His dear sake? Do we not long that all the hereditary proclivities of our nature may be corrected, chastened, refined, and made harmonious beneath His gentle sceptre?—and is not that the very miracle which we begin to find happening? Quite apart from theories of holiness, when we earnestly *love* Jesus, and are thercfoie gladly yielded to Him, the Holy Spirit has His gracious opportunity with us; He fills and sanctifies us, heart, mind, soul, spirit, without any need for excited beggings and pleadings and "claimings" on our part. In a word, when we earnestly *love* Him, everything else falls into its proper place, and our Lord suffuses us with His sanctifying Spirit.

Years ago, when I became minister of Bethesda Free Church, Sunderland, County Durham, I began to hear many appreciative remarks concerning a former deacon who had died a few years earlier. I was told that it was almost impossible to think or speak unworthily in his presence; that he always brought a sense of God's presence when he came into a room; and that in the office-bearers' meetings, if a discussion ever seemed to be getting edgy or uncharitable, he would quietly rise and lead the brethren in such a prayer that afterward the discussion could only continue on a high spiritual plane. He left a lovely influence lingering behind him, and I began to wish I had known him. He was Mr. W. T. Longstaff; and he wrote a hymn which gives us his secret; a hymn which is now well-known and often sung. Here it is: and it will be to our profit to read through it again thoughtfully:

> Take time to be holy,
>   Speak oft with thy Lord.
> Abide in Him always,
>   And feed on His word.
> Make friends of God's children;
>   Help those who are weak;
> Forgetting in nothing
>   His blessing to seek.
>
> Take time to be holy,
>   The world rushes on.
> Spend much time in secret
>   With Jesus alone.
> By looking to Jesus
>   Like Him thou shalt be;
> Thy friends in thy conduct
>   His likeness shall see.
>
> Take time to be holy,
>   Be calm in thy soul;
> Each thought and emotion
>   Beneath His control.
> Thus led of His spirit,
>   To fountains of love,
> Thou soon shalt be fitted
>   For service above.

When we earnestly *love* our Lord, we begin to live after the pattern of that hymn, and a Spirit-filled experience of practical sanctification becomes ours.

But, again, this matter of our love for Christ is basic and decisive in our *service* for Him. Some time ago I was chatting with a dear old saint who through many years has kept a loyal banner of Christian testimony waving in his town. He got to talking about his younger days and some of the fine young men who had started out with him in serving Christ but had later cooled off and given up. When I asked him the reason why some of the others had dropped out, he replied: "Ah, I think it was because they were spurred on by enthusiasm for a cause rather than constrained by real love for the Lord Jesus. They thought that the lodging-house work, and the open-air meetings, and other Gospel ventures, were just going to transform everything and everybody in quick-short time. Then, when steady opposition made the going heavy, they became dispirited, and gradually dropped out." There is a great deal in that dear old brother's words. The only thing which keeps us steadily persevering through the years, patiently persisting, and buoyantly overcoming discouragements, is to be doing it all out of *love for Him*.

That was the big, open secret of Paul's indomitable tenacity. "We are troubled on every side, yet not distressed; we are perplexed, but not in despair; persecuted, but not forsaken; cast down, but not destroyed; always bearing about in the body the dying of the Lord Jesus that the life also of Jesus might be made manifest in our body . . . *For the love of Christ constraineth us* . . ." (2 Cor. iv. 8–10, v. 14). The very thought of Christ's love had a continually constraining effect upon Paul. It caused him so to love Christ in return that he simply had to "keep at it" through good and ill, through success and through seeming failure. Oh, this is the grand motive which gives Christian service its sacred glory and highest meaning—that we do it out of love for *HIM*! And this is what gives us the most persevering resolution to keep on—that we do it out of love for *HIM*! And this is what gives our heavenly Master His richest pleasure in it—that we do it out of love for *HIM*!

Once again, this matter of our present love to Christ, while we are still here on earth, will have repercussions reaching right on into the *heavenly future* which is prepared for us. I believe that our Lord's second coming to this earth is now quickly drawing upon us. I believe that our Lord and our Christian departed in heaven anticipate their coming descent with "exceeding great joy". I believe that our Lord is coming for *all* those on earth who are truly His; and I reject the idea of a so-called "partial rapture". Yet, even so, our Lord evidently has special pleasure in those who are the more eagerly awaiting Him because they *love* Him, for Paul says, in 2 Timothy iv. 8, "Henceforth there is laid up for me a crown of righteousness, which the Lord, the righteous Judge, shall give me at that day; and not to me only, but unto all them also that *love* His appearing." This reminds us also of 1 Corinthians ii. 9, "Eye hath not seen, nor ear heard, neither have entered into the heart of man, the things which God hath prepared for them that *love* Him."

The greatest of all preparations for our Lord's coming and kingdom, and for those "ages to come" when he will show us the "exceeding riches of His grace in His kindness toward us" (Eph. ii. 7) is that we should *love* Him with all our heart and mind and soul and strength.

Well, just as it was *then*, more than nineteen hundred years ago, in the glistening light of that early morning by Galilee, as the scintillating wavelets lapped over the shingle, and the disciples sat at that unusual, never-to-be-forgotten breakfast with their risen Lord on the shore, so is it *now*, this very minute: our risen Lord asks you and me,

"LOVEST THOU ME?"

That is the question which goes deeper than all others. What is your reply? What is mine? Can we say with Simon Peter, "Lord, Thou knowest all things; Thou knowest that I love Thee"? If so, can we say it with Peter's depth of meaning, and with equal degree of affectionate devotion? Oh, think again what He has done for us! Think again who He is! Think again how we *ought* to love Him! Think again of all it can mean, both here and hereafter, if we love Him as our dearest Treasure! Oh, that these all-too-earthbound minds and hearts of ours might melt in gratitude and love and utter consecration to Him!

> Let me love Thee, Thou art claiming
>   Every feeling of my soul;
> Let that love, in power prevailing,
>   Render Thee my life's control.
> For life's burdens, they are easy,
>   And life's sorrows lose their sting,
> If they're carried all to please Thee;
>   If their pain Thy smile should bring.

LOVE IS THE GREATEST

Gracious Spirit, Holy Ghost,
Taught by Thee we covet most,
Of Thy gifts at Pentecost,
    Holy, heavenly love.

Prophecy will fade away,
Melting in the light of day;
Love will ever with us stay.
    Therefore give us love.

Faith and hope and love we see
Joining hand in hand agree;
But the greatest of the three,
    And the best, is love.

Bishop Christopher Wordsworth.

LOVE IS THE GREATEST

"And now abideth faith, hope, love, these three; and the greatest of these is love."—1 Cor. xiii. 13.

THIS thirteenth chapter of First Corinthians is the acknowledged classic on love. If we would most clearly grasp its truth we need to realise that it is not a separate entity, but the central section of an instructive and impressive dissertation on *spiritual gifts,* as we see in the chapter next before it, and the chapter next after it.

The Corinthians were infatuated, apparently, with the spectacular, making much ado about the more demonstrative gifts of the Spirit, particularly miracle-workings, speakings in tongues, and interpretings. This may have been due to their characteristic Corinthian temperament; but whether that was so or not, it was unhealthy. They tended to place false values on things, and to underestimate those more deeply spiritual and indispensable gifts of the Spirit which produce holiness of character.

That this was so is evident from the fact that despite their miracle-workings and speakings in tongues the spiritual state of the church was disappointing; nay, worse, it was seriously low, as the epistle reveals. Paul writes his letter to them, anxious to save them from an erratic, impulsive, superficial view of things; anxious to steady them, and give them a truer outlook. All the Spirit's gifts are good. All have their right place and true use to the glory of God; but some are much more important than others; and therefore the apostle counsels them in the last verse of chapter xii, "Covet earnestly the best gifts; and yet I show unto you the more excellent way." Then follows chapter xiii, in which the "more excellent way" is set before us. "Though I speak with the tongues (not only) of men, but (even) of angels," and though I do all manner of other extraordinary things, if I do not have *love* governing my motives and filling my heart, it is all morally valueless, it "profiteth me *nothing*".

And so this thirteenth chapter goes on, until in its last verse we find this final statement of the three things which are most fundamental, vital, and enduring: "And now abideth faith, hope, love, these three; but the greatest of these is love." The apostle, be it noted, says that all three are permanent, but one excels.

The Permanency of the Three

Again and again, in the New Testament, faith and hope and love are linked together. See 1 Thessalonians i, 3: "Remembering without ceasing your work of *faith* and labour of *love*, and patience of *hope*." See Colossians i. 4, 5: "Since we heard of your *faith* in Christ Jesus, and of the *love* which ye have to all the saints, and for the *hope* which is laid up for you in heaven." See 1 Peter i. 21, 22: "That your *faith* and *hope* might be in God . . . see that ye *love* one another with a pure heart fervently." See Galatians v. 5, 6: "We through the Spirit wait for the *hope* of righteousness by *faith* . . . which worketh by *love*."

The three are beautifully blended in the Communion Service or Observance of the Lord's Supper. The bread and wine symbolise the broken body and blood of Christ, and speak of the crucified Saviour who is the object of our *faith* for salvation. But as Paul says, "As often as ye eat this bread and drink this cup ye do show the Lord's death *until He come*", which speaks of the soon-returning Lord who is the object of our *hope* for future blessedness. Again, when our Lord Himself instituted the Supper, He said, "Do this in remembrance of Me", which speaks of the bodily absent Bridegroom who is the object of our *love*. In that sacred supper of remembrance, faith looks back to the Cross and is strengthened; love looks up to the Bridegroom and is deepened; hope looks on to the Rapture and is brightened.

"And now abideth faith, hope, love." These three are distinctively represented in the New Testament by the three main writers among the apostles. Paul is distinguishingly the writer on faith; Peter on hope; John on love. Moreover, the order in our text is the order of succession as the New Testament unfolds; for Paul comes first; then Peter; then John.

What is more, this is the normal order of Christian experience. The Christian life begins with faith on Christ. Then, with the new life comes new hope. Then, arising from a sense of salvation and God-given hope comes the first intelligently passionate response of love.

From all this, is it not clear that we are to regard faith, hope, love, as the three most fundamental qualities of the Christian life? Faith, hope, love, apart from all else, will save and sanctify and glorify any human soul. The action of *sin* in a human life produces the three opposites of faith, hope, love, namely, unbelief, despair, hatred.

Our text says, "And now *abideth* faith, hope, love." I am glad that these three abide. There are so many things which do *not* abide—youth, health, opportunity, privileges, friends, loved ones. Gradually, inevitably, sometimes all too quickly, how do the choicest possessions pass from us on the ever-rolling stream of time! That thrilling new book, that entrancing new song, that fascinating new philosophy, that dazzling new star, how quickly their apparent immortality wears off! How surely their appeal dies with the lapse of years! How soon they fade into forgottenness! But faith and hope and love abide; they *can* abide, and they *do* abide, and they *will* abide, and they *must* abide, because *HE* abides, who is the perfect embodiment of love, and the supreme object of faith, and the undisappointing fulfiller of highest human hope; "Jesus Christ, the same yesterday, and today, and forever" (Heb. xiii. 8).

Yes, the text says, "And now *abideth* faith, hope, love." Mark the contrast here with verse 8: "Whether there be prophecies, they shall fail; whether there be tongues, they shall cease; whether there be knowledge, it shall vanish away." Those peculiar, supernatural efflorescences of early Christianity are not indispensable to true holiness of character, and therefore they are not the imperishably permanent components of Christianity. All our teachings ("prophecies"), and all our speakings ("tongues"), and all our knowings ("knowledge") are not so important as our *character;* and character is determined by the place of faith, hope, and love in the heart and life.

"And now *abideth* faith, hope, love." Here is a singular verb with a plural subject. It would seem at first as though Paul should have written, "And now *abide* faith, hope, love"; but no, he must needs use the singular, "abideth", because faith, hope, love, are a trinity in unity. They can be easily distinguished from each other but never separated from each other. If we have true *faith* we also have *love,* for as Galatians v. 6 says, "faith worketh by love". If we have *love,* we also have *hope,* for as Romans v. 5 says, "Hope maketh not ashamed because the love of God is shed abroad in our hearts." These three agree in one.

Notice, too, that the verb, "abideth", *applies to all three,* not just to love, as some have said. There is a sense, admittedly, in which, at the translation of the Church and the rapture of the saints, faith and hope will be superseded by fulfilment. Faith will be lost in sight, and hope consummated in realisation. Yet there is a richer and greater sense in which faith and hope will live on through "the ages to come". Think carefully: what do we mean when we say that faith and hope will be done away as needless in heaven? We only mean that *one aspect* of faith and hope will be done away. If we think of faith simply as belief in the unseen, then certainly, when we are actually *there,* in the "land that is fairer than day", we shall see that which we formerly believed in without seeing, and faith will melt away in the light of visible reality. But faith in the sense of its being trust and repose in Christ, and a resting in the enjoyment of Him, will live on for ever—ever deepening and enriching us. Faith is permanent, and in heaven it will be perfect.

Similarly, *hope* will live on through the ages. In this present life, when we Christians speak of our glorious hope in Christ, we generally have in mind a future state of bliss which has been promised. But when that glory dawns on us, and we stand amid the excellences of "fairer worlds on high", will hope be over? No; heaven will be a place of golden dreams which will all come true; a place where every longing will have a fulfilling; a succession of glad sunrises, without one sunset of frustration. With every hope realised, glowing new expectancies will be kindled in the heart. We cannot enjoy all heaven at once. There will always be more to look forward to; always lovelier new horizons; and we shall have the restful joy of anticipation without the faintest fear of disappointment. Ever-renewed hope and ever-satisfying fulfilments will go on and on in complementary alternation.

Both faith and hope will be perfected in heaven, because *love* is also perfect there. Love will be the very atmosphere of heaven's undying rapture. Perfect love creates perfect faith and expels all fear. Perfect love is itself the heaven which fulfils all that is dearest and truest and highest in hope. Yes, all three are permanent; our text is true: "And now abideth faith, hope, love."

The Supremacy of the One

The text, however, goes on to add, "But the greatest of these is love." I seem to remember that in my boyhood days, the Methodist preachers who used to "hold forth" in our church and mission hall placed the main emphasis on *faith*. It was faith which saved the soul. Faith was the first-required and first-in-order of the virtues. Whatever else one might have, "without faith" it was "impossible to please God" or to achieve "exploits". What we all needed was faith.

Perhaps we all need to pray, "Lord increase our faith"; yet as the late Professor Henry Drummond sent echoing round the Scottish universities, "The greatest thing in the world is *love*." It is the greatest thing in *any* world. It is not without peculiar interest that it is Paul (distinctively the apostle of faith) who avers, in our text, "The greatest of these is love."

But *how* is love greater than faith and hope? Well, first of all, it is nobler, higher, greater, because it is distinguishingly the *social* virtue of the great trio. Faith saves *me*. Hope cheers *me*. Love serves *others*. Faith appropriates something for *myself*. Hope anticipates something for *myself*. Love sends me out of myself in gracious concern for *others*.

> Love ever gives, forgives, outlives;
> And ever stands with open hands.
> For while love gives, it lives;
> And while love lives, it gives.
> Yea, this is love's prerogative
> To give—and give—and give.

Next, love is that moral quality which gives their moral value to all the other virtues. Where love is absent, all other so-called virtues lose their real worth and lustre. "Though I speak with the tongues of men and of angels, and have not love, I am become as sounding brass, or a tinkling cymbal. And though I have the gift of prophecy, and understand all mysteries, and all knowledge; and though I have all faith, so that I could remove mountains, and have not love, I am *nothing*. And though I bestow all my goods to feed the poor, and though I give my body to be burned, and have not love, it profiteth me *nothing*." Love is the queen of the virtues. Pure love is that state which comprises in itself true holiness and godlikeness.

Again, love is the *end* to which all the other virtues and graces are means. Love is not a stepping-stone to something higher; but all other moral excellences are meant to be stepping-stones to love.

Furthermore, faith and hope are states which pertain to creatures merely, whereas love finds its place in the heart of the Creator Himself. The Eternal One does not merely believe or hope, as we dependent beings need to do; but He *does* have and express this wonderful quality or emotion which we call *love*. Nowhere does the Scripture say, "God is faith", or "God is hope"; but it does say, "God is *love*"—and never did so short a sentence contain a vaster or sublimer truth.

Then again, love is God's supreme manifestation of Himself to mankind in His incarnate Son. Love was the motive in that miraculous advent of two millenniums ago. Love was the predominant feature of that incomparable life and ministry on earth. Love was the master-passion of that tragic yet wondrous Cross.

In consonance with all this, love is now our Lord's special *law* for His people. "Bear ye one another's burdens, and so fulfil the law of Christ" (Gal. vi. 2). "Fulfil the royal law. . . . Thou shalt love thy neighbour as thyself" (Jas. ii. 8). "A new commandment give I unto you, That ye love one another, as I have loved you" (John xiii. 34).

Just once more, love blends all the interests of God, and of the unfallen angels, and of all the redeemed, into one. In heaven, perfect love will unite all in one unending harmony and felicity. I believe there is good Scripture ground for holding that heaven is a *place*, not just a condition; but I am equally sure that the pure rapture of heaven is the by-product of love, not just of celestial surroundings, however glorious they may be.

How can love be anything less than supreme if this thirteenth chapter of First Corinthians is its photograph? Oh, this wonderful, exquisite, delectable, practical, sublime quality which suffers long and is kind, never envies, never boasts, is never conceited, never behaves unseemly, is utterly unselfish, always seeking other's good, is gentle tempered, pure minded, never rejoices in evil, but always rejoices in the virtuous, beareth all things, believeth all things, hopeth all things, endureth all things, and "never faileth"! Tested by 1 Corinthians xiii, how little love there is in some of us! How self-preoccupied we are! How little real generosity, magnanimity, forgivingness, or self-denying "otherism" there is! Love is the great need among us. I sometimes think that if church membership were decided by this Corinthian chapter there would scarcely be any of us left on the rolls! D. L. Moody once said that if a man ever opened a shop as a photographer of hearts he would soon be bankrupt!

One of the lovely wonders about our Lord Jesus is, that if we go through this thirteenth chapter of First Corinthians changing the word "love" to the name, "Jesus", in each place where the word "love" occurs, it reads absolutely truly of Him. Read verses 4 to 8, and see how this is so.

Could *you* go through those verses, putting *your* name in where the word "love" occurs? Could I? Are we too ashamed, too impatient, too resigned to our littleness? Oh, let us look through the golden gates of this chapter again, not only seeing the shining upland to which they lead, but realising that there is a secret spring which opens the gates of possibility for us! That same Jesus whose name fits every description of love *lives within us,* if we are truly His people! When *He* lives within us, *love* lives within us. When we let Him control us and fill us, true love, divine love, dominates us and communicates itself through us.

This is that highest and richest and biggest of blessings which all Christian hearts should be seeking, yea, and proving in sanctifying reality. The greatest gift that the Holy Spirit can impart to us is not the power to speak in tongues, or to interpret, or to heal the sick, or to work "signs", but to make us truly *loving.* All the other things, apart from love, are not only morally valueless, they are dangerous. The greatest miracle of the Holy Spirit is to make an ugly life beautiful, a stingy heart generous, a jealous covetor magnanimous, a self-centred grasper Christ-like, a hateful mind loving. We may be *filled* with that Holy Spirit, who is the Spirit of Christ. But the fullness of the Spirit was never designed to give us some weird, uncanny power to do startling things, nor to give us some unnatural atmosphere about our personalities. No; the Spirit fills us that we may be filled with the very love of Jesus Himself. This is no mere sentimental, vapoury kind of love. It is *real* love. It makes missionaries, not mere visionaries. It is practical, not just mystical. It expresses itself in doing, not just in dreaming. Where there is trouble, it not only weeps, it works; it not only hopes, it helps. Away with counterfeits! We want the real thing, and this is it! I remember again a prayer which I once heard a Methodist preacher pray years ago: "Lord, make us intensely spiritual; but keep us perfectly natural, and thoroughly practical." That is always what happens where there is a genuine filling of heart by the Holy Spirit, the Spirit of our Lord Jesus Christ, the Spirit of love.

I also recall a prayer which has been handed down from St. Francis of Assisi, which, in the form of a prayer addressed to our Lord, describes what happens when the love of Christ fills the heart and transforms the life:

> Lord, make me a channel of Thy life;
> That where there is hatred I may bring love;
> That where there is wrong I may bring forgiveness;
> That where there is discord I may bring harmony;
> That where there is error I may bring truth;
> That where there is doubt I may bring faith;
> That where there is despair I may bring hope;
> That where there are shadows I may bring light;
> That where there is sadness I may bring joy.
> May I seek rather to comfort than to be comforted;
> To understand than to be understood;
> To love rather than to be loved.
> For it is by giving that I receive;
> It is by self-forgetting that I find;
> It is by forgiving that I am forgiven;
> It is by dying that I awake to life indeed.

Oh, to be really filled with the life and love of Christ! After all our exegesis and theorising, what *is* practical holiness? It is *love* filling the heart and overflowing through the life. True, intelligent love to Christ never makes escapist recluses, cloistered monks or unpractical mystics; nay, it makes compassionate and active benefactors, who forget themselves in serving others, and who in so doing find the very joy of heaven thrilling in their hearts. Yes, the secret of true joy is the "otherism" of love!

Part Three: ABOUT SERVING HIM

Thus far, these meditations have concerned themselves with our knowing and loving Christ. But even as knowing is meant to develop into loving, so both knowing and loving are to issue in serving. It is the very nature of love to serve. What, then, is service for Christ? What is its basic nature? What is its highest or most potent expression? What is its main aim? What is its creative motive? What are its requirements or conditions of effectiveness? To answer these questions amply could fill many chapters. Never was there more widespread, well-meaning, highly organised religious activity than today; yet how much of it is truly service for Christ according to the New Testament standard? With an allusion to the epic Charge of the Light Brigade, a famous missionary blended humour and satire when he exclaimed, "Canons to the right of us, bishops to the left of us, preachers all around us, volley and thunder", and then asked how much it all accomplished. How much so-called Christian service is in the "energy of the flesh"! How much is service for institutional Christianity rather than for Christ Himself! How much is a going round in circles, or like rivers losing themselves in the sands! How complicated the originally simple has become! What intermingling sincerity, vagueness, and misunderstanding there is! What most of us are needing to reconsider is that outside the will of Christ there may be much activity but there can be no service. We need also to lay well to heart the following four axioms. (1) Spiritual service is being rather than doing. (2) Its ruling motive must be love to Christ. (3) It must be Christ-directed and Spirit-endued. (4) Its first priority is soul-winning, and its mightiest weapon is prayer.

"Life is built a day at a time; and the Scriptures keep this constantly in view in their promises. So, Christian, tired and somewhat disheartened, take the Lord a day at a time. Let the life-time you deal with be just for today; and for *today* you possess nothing less than THE WHOLE CHRIST OF GOD!"

Bishop Handley Moule.

THE FOUR TRANSES

"I live, yet not I, but Christ liveth in me, and the life which I now live in the flesh I live by the faith of the Son of God, who loved me, and gave Himself for me."
—Gal. ii. 20.

WITH these immortal words of Paul before us, we may say that the Christian life, as taught in the New Testament, consists of four *transes:* (1) transition, (2) transfusion, (3) transmission, (4) translation. In these days of much vague thinking on the Christian life, it is the more important that we should keep this fourfold view of it clearly in mind. Eternal issues are bound up in it.

Transition

That prepositionary prefix, *trans,* always denotes a crossing over from one place or condition to another place or condition. There is an *out of* and an *into*. It can never be too often emphasised that the true Christian life begins with a supernatural, spiritual *transition*. Paul indicates this in his words, "I live, yet not I." The old "Saul" has given place to the new "Paul". This initial transition is commonly called "conversion". Every real conversion to Christ is nothing less than a gracious divine interposition in some human personality whereby a regenerating transition is effected. This is equally true, whether conversion occurs with volcanic suddenness or as the outcome of a process as gradual as day-dawn. There is a coming *out of* and a passing *into*.

In our New Testament, we find a fascinating variety of metaphors used to express this transition which we call conversion. Let me here pick out just three; one from Peter, one from Paul, and one from our Lord Himself.

Take Peter's. That sturdy apostle, being an outdoor man, takes his metaphors from the realm of nature. Thus, in speaking of conversion, he says, "Show forth the praises of Him who hath called you out of *darkness* into His marvellous *light*" (1 Pet. ii. 9). What a transition *that* is! Darkness and light are sheer opposites. Yet Peter's figure of speech is no mere poetic exaggeration or extravagant hyperbole. He was referring to something indubitably real in the experience of those to whom he wrote, as the pronoun, "you", indicates. Even so, every true conversion to Christ is nothing less than a coming out of gross natural "darkness" into a marvellous new spiritual "light"—a transforming new discovery of God, and a world of spiritual realities unknown before.

When we turn from Peter to Paul, we are in the presence of a very different mental type. Paul was forensically minded. His was the lawyer-mind among the apostolic band. As often as not, when Paul wants a metaphor he goes to the law court. So, when *he* speaks of coversion, he pictures it to us as a *legal* transaction, a coming out of *"condemnation"* into a wonderful new Godward standing which he calls *"justification"* in Christ.

Perhaps the most remarkable of all metaphors to express this conversion-transition is that which our Lord Himself uses in John v. 24: "Verily, verily, I say unto you, He that heareth my word, and believeth on Him that sent Me, hath everlasting life, and shall not come into condemnation, but is passed from *death* unto *life*." That is the sheerest transition of all. We cannot be a bit dead and a bit alive! We may be in a poor state of health, but if we are alive we are not dead, and once we are dead we are no longer alive! That is true not only physically, but spiritually. Every one of us is either spiritually alive to God in Christ, or spiritually dead "in trespasses and sins" (Eph. ii. 1). When by simple but vital faith we become savingly united to God's dear Son, there occurs nothing less than a transition from spiritual death to new spiritual life!

What a wonderful transition, then, conversion to Christ is!— from darkness to light; from condemnation to justification; from death to life. There is a dear old hymn—one of my favourites in the old Sankey twelve-hundred edition, which is all about this transition. I quote just the first verse.

> *Out of* my bondage, sorrow and night,
> Jesus, I come; Jesus, I come.
> *Into* Thy freedom, gladness and light,
> Jesus, I come to Thee.

Out of my sickness, *into* Thy health;
Out of my want, and *into* Thy wealth;
Out of my sin, and *into* Thyself;
        Jesus I come to Thee.

Transfusion

Take, now, the second of our four transes. The true Christian
life, which begins with a supernatural transition, consists and
continues in a supernatural *transfusion*. The very life and nature
of Christ are transfused into the inmost being of the Christian
believer by the Holy Spirit. Thus our Saviour's word is fulfilled:
"Because I live, ye shall live also" (John xiv. 19). Paul not only
says, "I live, yet not I"; he goes on to say, "but *Christ liveth
in me.*" There is not only transition; there is transfusion.

This is the most precious and sacred secret of the Christian
life: "Christ liveth in me." The man of the world neither under-
stands it nor even suspects it. "The world knoweth us not" (1 John
iii. 1). Yet oh, how real it is to our Lord's own! "Christ *in*
you, the hope of glory" (Col. i. 27).

Now just because of this supernatural transfusion, the New
Testament ideal for our Christian life is that there shall be within
us a continual displacement of the old self-life, and an ever-clearer
enthronement of the new Christ-life. All of us, by nature, are
egocentric, self-centred; but we are meant to become Christocentric, or Christ-centred. Christ is to be the new life within our
life; the new mind within our mind; the new will within our
will; the new love within our love; the new Person within our
personality. "Christ liveth in me."

We cannot always be on the mountain top of transfiguration,
seeing heavenly visions and hearing heavenly voices. We cannot
always be experiencing spiritual raptures and sensory ecstasies.
A high frequency of these is neither necessary nor desirable in
our present state; nor could our nervous system sustain too much
of it. Often we must be down on the long-stretching plains of
every-day hum-drum realities; and sometimes we must needs be
down in some grim valley, drawing the sword in fierce battle
against Apollyon himself. Yet whether up on the mountain top,
or down on the monotonous plain, or deep in some valley of trial,
I am convinced of this, that we Christian believers need never

lose an uninterrupted consciousness of our indwelling Saviour. Surely this is implied in the words, "Christ liveth in me." To be Christocentric is to be all the while Christ-conscious.

The whole of our consciousness is meant to be interpenetrated with the consciousness of *His* indwelling life and mind and will and love, even as the air in Summer is transfused with sunshine. At conferences for the deepening of the spiritual life I have sometimes heard speakers say that the "self" in us must die. I do not wish to seem unduly critical, but surely that is an overstatement of what the Scripture teaches. Actually, the "self" is the very *ego*, the basic, thinking entity which constitutes personal being. For the "self" to die, therefore, is nothing less than annihilation of the very personality. What the Scripture *does* teach is that the whole of the human "self" is to be sublimated in the life of our indwelling Lord, so that self-consciousness becomes continually blended with Christ-consciousness. Dear Christian, whom I now address, which is the more prominent in *your* experience, self-consciousness or Christ-consciousness? Do *you* carry with you, all the time, a lovely, clinging awareness of *Him*?

Far too many Christians live their spiritual life on the *"battery system"*. Lest that sounds a strangely peculiar idea, let me explain at once what I mean. I can dimly remember how, when I was a very little boy, my dear mother sometimes took me to a town where, if I remember rightly, about that time there was a change-over in the street-car system. The older type of street-car used to run on the battery system. There was an electric battery on the front or rear platform of the car, and so long as the battery was "alive" the car would run; but as soon as the battery was exhausted, the car would stop dead. It was far from satisfactory, hence the change-over. Now there are Christian believers who seem to run their spiritual life and service on that system. They go to a convention on the deeper life, and oh, when they return, they are altogether different—for three weeks! Or they read some epochal Christian biography, and as they close the book they say, "Ah, life can never be the same again"; nor is it—for three weeks! Or they have an all-night of prayer. Things have been going from bad to worse with them, so they bring things to a crisis. While others sleep, they wrestle on the banks of their nocturnal brook Jabbok (Gen. xxxii. 22), and when the sun rises they are transfigured—for three weeks, after which they lapse again to the dull average. Why? Because they are resting on a *crisis* instead of on *Christ*.

The Christian life was never meant to run on the battery system. It was meant to run on the *electric circuit principle*. You know what that is. Put simply, it is just this: continuous *current* through continuous *contact*. You and I have no power over the current; but we do have power over the contact; and when, by regular prayer-times, daily meditation in the written Word, consecration to Christ, and separation from unworthy ways, we maintain the "contact", then the heavenly current, the Holy Spirit, the life of Christ, is continuously communicated to us. Thus, as the hymn says,

> Moment by moment I'm kept in His love,
> Moment by moment I've *life* from above.

Transmission

Look now at the third of our four transes. The Christian life, which originates in a supernatural transition, and consists in a supernatural transfusion, is meant to express itself by an equally supernatural *transmission*. It is most important to get right on this point, for it raises the whole question as to what Christian *service* is. Moreover, many well-meaning believers easily mislead themselves in this connection. There are many who seem to think that Christian service consists in indefatigable doing, doing, doing. No. Fundamentally, Christian service is *being,* rather than doing; though doing, of course, is meant to be the completive *expression* of being. In Christian service it is more than ever true that quality is more than quantity. What I *am* is far more than what I say or even do. The highest and greatest service which I can ever render to Christ is not that which *I* do *for* Him, but that which I allow Him to do *through* me. Christian service, in essence, is Christ-communicativeness.

This is surely what Paul has in mind when he adds, "And the life which I now live *in the body*, I live by faith in the Son of God, who loved me, and gave Himself for me." No longer does Paul live on the old principle of self-determination, not even in serving Christ. He now lives and serves on the new principle of Christ-occupation and Christ-direction. He lives continually by faith in the Son of God, which communicates the new life not only *to* him, but *through* him. Fundamentally, this world does not need you or me, and when we pass hence it will get on without us; but it desperately needs *HIM*; and in the economy of redemption *He* needs *you* and *me* as consecrated personalities through whom He can communicate His grace and life and love to others. He does not ask merely for my physical activity, or even for my mental productivity; He wants my total *conductivity*. He does not call me to be a creator, but a *transmitter*.

If I may refer to my boyhood days again, I remember how, again and again, my dear mother would softly sing the following verse before going out to her preaching appointments:

> Oh, to be nothing, nothing,
>   Simply to lie at Thy feet;
> A broken and emptied vessel
>   For my Master's use made meet!
> Emptied, that Thou mayest fill me,
>   As forth to Thy service I go;
> Emptied, that so, unhindered
>   Thy life through mine might flow.

Oh, that is it—"Emptied that so, unhindered, *Thy* life through *mine* might flow"!

After the comparatively small but indomitable British airforce had broken the might and humbled the pride of the German Luftwaffe in the world war of 1939 to 1945, Winston Churchill broadcast the memorable words, "Never did so many owe so much to so few." Likewise, in these days, when so *many* in our churches leave so *much* to be done by so *few*, there can be real danger to the "willing horses" who do all the pulling. Christian service can be either overwork or overflow. If it is the former, then sooner or later there comes an unhappy reaction of physical weariness, mental jadedness, nervous exhaustion, and sometimes even spiritual recoil. This is just what our subtle enemy desires and gloats over. But it is just what our kind Master intended should never be. Are we under Law, or under Grace? Is our Master an Egyptian slave-driver, or is He the King of Love? Do we serve Him because we *must,* or because we *may*? Did He send us to war at our own charges, or did He not say, "Tarry . . . until ye be endued with power from on high"?

Christian service is meant to be a continual inflow . . . overflow . . . outflow . . . onflow, of our heavenly Master's very life in us and through us. When that is our secret, there is a freshness and poise and buoyancy and ease about our serving which in itself is a contagious happiness from heaven. It is then that we know how true are the words, "The joy of the Lord is your strength" (Neh. viii. 10). We are continually replenished from secret springs and hidden sources which are a mystery to the uninitiated, but are a superb reality to those who by prayer and faith and love dwell deep in Christ.

So, then, whatever outward forms it takes, Christian service, fundamentally, is transmitting Christ. Some years ago, in an old Anglican church, in an English village-town, an elderly clergyman was almost at the end of a very ordinary sermon to a rather drowsy little congregation, when he suddenly livened up and in electric tones shouted a sentence which still rings in our memory: "Oh, my friends, the greatest of all things in life is to know the living Christ in your own heart, and to be able to communicate Him to others!" Never was a truer thing said. Miss Beatrice Cleland has immortalised it in her deft poemette, which I believe she wrote as a tribute to the person who led her to the Saviour:

> Not only by the words you say,
> Not only in your deeds confessed,
> But in the most unconscious way
>   Is Christ expressed.
>
> Is it a beatific smile,
> Or holy light upon your brow?
> Oh no, I felt His presence while
>   You laughed just now.
>
> For me 'twas not the truth you taught,
> To you so clear, to me so dim,
> But when *you* came to me you brought
>   A sense of *Him*.
>
> And from your eyes *He* beckons me,
> And from your lips *His* love is shed,
> Till I lose sight of you, and see
>   The Christ instead.

Translation

And now, glance, even though only momentarily, at the last of our four transes. The Christian life, which, as we have said, originates in a supernatural transition, and continues by a supernatural transfusion, and expresses itself through a supernatural transmission, is to be consummated in a supernatural *translation*.

What is the deepmost or ultimate purpose of God in saving us through His Redeemer-Son? Is it that we might escape the damnation of Gehenna, where the worm never dies and the flame is never quenched? Well, whatever that doom may be, to be saved is to be saved from that, thank God! Yet that is not the fundamental purpose of God in saving us. Is it, then, that we might enjoy the "many mansions" of the Father's house, and an "eternal weight of glory" through coming ages? Well, whatever heights of bliss are indicated in such resplendent phraseology, to be saved means to be saved to that! Yet neither is that the deepest intent of God in redeeming us.

If we would know what it is, e must turn to Romans viii. 28, 29—"And we know that all things work together for good to them that love God, who are the called according to His *purpose*." (It is the whole sweep of the divine *purpose* which is here in view.) "For whom He did foreknow (i.e. in the eternal past), He also did predestinate (i.e. in the eternal future) to be *CONFORMED TO THE IMAGE OF HIS SON,* that He might be the firstborn among many brethren." So the ultimate purpose of God in our salvation is that at last we shall be presented "before the presence of His glory" as the exact *replicas* of His dear Son, that He might be "the firstborn among *many* brethren" all bearing His likeness! Why, this is also the very last picture which the Bible gives us of the raptured saints amid the future glories of the new heaven and the new earth: "And they shall see His face; and *His name shall be in their foreheads*" (Rev. xxii. 4); which is simply a beautiful, symbolical way of saying they will all be so like Him that when you look at *them* you will see *Him,* whom they now perfectly reflect.

Even here and now, in this life on earth, there ought to be a growing likeness to Him in our character, so that others take knowledge of us that we have "been with Jesus". God grant that such likeness to Him there may be! But, oh, that golden morning which brings our Bridegroom-King back to us! May it haste "over the mountains of Bether"! "Beloved, now are we the sons of God, and it doth not yet appear what we shall be; but we know that when *He* shall appear, *we* shall be *LIKE HIM*, for we shall see Him as He is" (1 John iii. 2).

In an earlier part of these devotional studies we have ventured to express our sincere disapproval of the growing tendency to display (and often to revere sentimentally) artists' paintings of what our Lord is supposed to have looked like when He was here on earth. The most popular of these, especially in America, seems to be Sallman's "Head of Christ". I am not denying that the face is a noble one, betokening a lovely manhood, even though it is not the suggested likeness of Christ which has most appealed to my own imagination. It has gained wide vogue. We see it hanging in many a ministers' office or vestry, in a great many Protestant churches, and in nearly every Sunday School. Yes, it is noble-looking and attractive, but the more widely and exclusively it fastens this one concept of our Lord's likeness in Christian minds, the more misleading and even dangerous it becomes. The fact is (let us emphasize it again) that we simply *do not know* what he was like in face and feature; and it is unwise to assume *any* fixed idea of His human appearance.

If we could get an authentic likeness of Him as He was in the long-ago, would even *that* be the picture of Him on which we should fix our eyes? Remember that although in one sense our Lord is just the same now as when He was on earth, in another sense He is greatly different. At His resurrection and heavenly exaltation a glorifying metamorphosis transfigured His human body. He is *not* now as He *was* in the days of His earthly sojourn, and therefore *no* picture or engraving can represent Him as He now is, with that supernal body and glory-flashing countenance. The apostle John distinctly informs us that when our Lord reappears at His second advent we shall *not* see Him as He *was*, but "as He *is*".

All over-absorption with the "Jesus of history" which detracts from the risen, living, ever-present Christ of experience, and the soon-returning Christ of glory, is a subtle snare. What measureless disservice the Roman church has done in fastening the eyes of millions on a Christ of the crucifix! He is no longer on the

Cross, for He said, "It is finished". Nor is He in the grave, for the angel said, "He is not here; He is risen". Let us try to think of Him "as He *is*", for that is how we are soon to see Him!

The climactic wonder is, that instantly upon seeing Him "as He is", we shall become "like him". The very seeing of Him is to effect the instantaneous transfiguration of His translated people into His own image. We are hearing much in these days about death-rays, asphyxiation rays, X-rays and other therapeutic rays. May it not be that when our Lord returns, our sudden, supernalising transfiguration may be effected by the intense glory-rays which emanate from His ineffable person? Like the bright sheen of sun-shafts piercing through the atmosphere, so the suddenly interpenetrating rays from the flaming splendour of the divine Son will immediately immortalise us.

Oh, the wonder of it! What a prospect! Read the perpetually surprising words again: "Beloved, now are we the sons of God, and it doth not yet appear what we shall be; but we know that when He shall appear, we shall be LIKE HIM, for we shall see Him AS HE IS"!

> As a flash of lightning, sudden, vivid, clear.
> Robed in whelming splendour will our Lord appear.
> One electric second!—Lo, the saints are *there*—
> Caught away to greet Him, in the shining air!
> In an eye's swift twinkling, at His advent shout.
> Skyward swept to see Him, changed within, without,
> Instantly we "see" Him, "like Him" we shall be;
> Then, our heaven for ever— His dear face to see!

SECRETS OF SUCCESS

There is a life in the will of Christ, so quiet, so at peace with God, so at rest in His joy, so perfectly content that He is doing the best, that the lines in the face are smoothed out; the fever is gone from the restless eye; and the whole nature is still. *Rest* in the Lord. Wait patiently for Him. *Then* spend in helping others from *your own experience.*

F. B. Meyer.

SECRETS OF SUCCESS

*"Cast the net on the right side of the ship and ye shall
find."*—John xxi. 6.

ALL of us who have found cleansing from sin through the precious
blood of Christ, and have become "born anew" by the Holy
Spirit, long to be true servants of our Lord and Saviour. We
have seen a glorious face which the world has never seen. We
have heard a thrilling voice which the world has never heard. We
have found a Saviour-Friend whom the world has never known.
We have enlisted in a service which the world does not understand. We have become the willing bond-slaves of God's dear
Son. He has said to us, "Follow Me, and I will make you fishers
of men." Above all else, we long to bring others to Him, that they
too may be eternally saved.

It is inevitable, therefore, that we find ourselves asking such
questions as: Where would Jesus have me go? What would
Jesus have me do? How would Jesus have me serve? Whom
would Jesus have me seek? What would Jesus have me give?
In which way, either generally or particularly, can I best serve
my heavenly Master?

Some are called to full-time service as ministers or evangelists
or missionaries or deaconesses or official administrators. Most of
us, however, can give only our spare time to specifically religious
activity; though of course there is a real sense in which we are
always "on duty" for Christ, through all the hours of what, either
rightly or wrongly, we call "secular" toil. But whether we are in
full-time Christian service or not, we are called to be witnesses
for Him; and one thing which we all should keep constantly
in mind is that our *highest* service, even as it is ever the most
urgent, is the *winning of souls to Him.* This is the highest
function we can ever fulfil toward another human being; and
if we would bring joy to the heart of our Lord, by successfully
winning, or helping to win others to Him, we need to grasp

clearly certain of the spiritual principles involved in effective service.

With this in mind, let us look again at that well-known paragraph in John xxi where we read of a fishing expedition which ended in dismal failure, but was afterward turned into the most surprising success. The paragraph runs as follows:

"After these things Jesus shewed Himself again to the disciples at the sea of Tiberias; and on this wise shewed He Himself. There were together Simon Peter, and Thomas called Didymus, and Nathaniel of Cana in Galilee, and the sons of Zebedee, and two other of His disciples. Simon Peter saith unto them, I go a fishing. They say unto him, We also go with thee. They went forth, and entered into a ship immediately; and that night they caught nothing. But when the morning was now come, Jesus stood on the shore: but the disciples knew not that it was Jesus. Then Jesus saith unto them, Children, have ye any meat? They answered Him, No. And He said unto them, Cast the net on the right side of the ship, and ye shall find. They cast therefore, and now they were not able to draw it for the multitude of fishes." (John xxi. 1–6.)

Fix on that third verse for a few minutes: "Simon Peter saith unto them, I go a fishing. They say unto him, we also go with thee. They went forth, and entered into a ship immediately; and that night they caught nothing." In that verse we see a sad but true illustration of what we may call self-conducted or self-managed service. It portrays what always happens when we essay to achieve spiritual results by our own cleverness, in our own strength, or according to our own supposed wisdom. It throws up a striking contrast between *self*-directed service (to which we are all prone) and *Christ*-directed service (the secret of which we all need to learn and constantly practice).

Self-Directed Service

"*I go a fishing.*" The words look innocent enough in themselves, yet somehow there is a ring of the old Simon-Peter *ego* about them. Are we over-imaginative in thinking so? Scarcely. The very way in which the words are recorded, taken with what follows, suggests Peter-like self-sure, almost heady tones.

Pause and reflect: Peter and his companions had earlier left those nets and boats at the call of Christ, to become fishers of men. For two years or more they had been going where *He* sent them, and doing what *He* directed. He had already met them twice since His astonishing reappearance from the grave (John xxi. 14); but there was nothing from Him about their going back to the old fishing business. When Peter said, "I go a fishing", did he mean simply for an odd night?—or was he opening a return-door to the past? We cannot conclusively settle which; but one thing is clear: it was a purely self-originated excursion, and one which unsuspectedly involved momentous issues, as we shall see.

If our Christian service is to be truly "Christian" and spiritually successful, then besides human *willingness* there must be divine *guidedness*. Peter had plenty of the former, but did not tarry to make sure of the latter. There is that same Peter-streak in all of us. Nothing is more important than to make sure that we are not serving our Lord (or rather, *supposedly* serving Him) in self-will, or according to our own poor, self-wisdom. We have said it before, and we repeat it for emphasis: Outside the will of Christ there may be much that is *called* Christian service, but there is no *real* Christian service; for real Christian service is the obedient fulfilment of *His will,* and nothing else, however well-meaning. There is such a thing as prayerless keenness to serve Him. It often looks fine; it has verve and dash; it makes tarrying for prayer seem a waste of valuable time; but oh, what blunderings! What needless giving of offence! What rush instead of rest! What noise instead of depth! What doubtful spiritual results compared with what *might* have been, with far less puff and steam and obtrusiveness!

"I go a fishing." But Peter did not go alone. The other half-dozen immediately responded, *"We also go with thee."* So here is not only a picture of service in self-will, but of service under *human leadership.* By a sort of common consent Peter's leadership was taken for granted. He dominated. He was made that way. Such human leadership can be of fine strategic advantage, but it becomes a snare whenever it veers away from the super-control of our heavenly Commander-in-Chief.

We must ever be careful not to follow human leaders in any way which would lead us away from the will of Christ for ourselves *individually.* God has His human champions to lead His people, His Joshuas and Samuels and Davids. Our Lord Jesus has His subordinate officers; His Pauls and Peters and Johns and others. We must rally to their standards and clarions, follow them and support them, yet never in a way which is inconsistent with the will of Christ as revealed to us each in particular; and never in a way which infringes on our direct, individual obedience to Christ.

But look again at this twenty-first chapter of John, and see the *impulsiveness* of self-directed service. "I go a fishing." "We also go with thee." "They went forth and entered into a ship *immediately*." The idea caught on like fire in dry timber. Never were a chairman and committee more unanimous. Neither need nor time for a word of prayer! Never a question, "Is it wise?" or "Ought we act so hastily?" or "Do you think *HE* might not wish us to spend the night out on the water?" or "Is the weather likely to be dangerous?" No; they went *"immediately"*.

Little did they realise that in launching out so impetuously they were endangering millions of souls! Satan would gleefully have sent that little barque to the bottom of the sea. It contained seven men—Peter, Thomas, Nathaniel, John, James, and two others, who had in their possession redeeming facts sufficient to "turn the world upside down" and save millions of souls. This, however, had not as yet dawned upon them; and all unknowingly they put the very Church of Christ in jeopardy by their impulsive action! They had yet to learn that in service for their risen Master, prayerless *rush* is foolish *risk*. There is always peril of one kind or another in self-willed service, whether at the time we realise it or not. Often we can do more harm than good. The secret of "safety, certainty, and enjoyment" in our Christian service is to wait to know His will.

Perhaps, however, that which is most of all pathetic and important to notice in the incident is the *result* of self-directed service. "They went forth and entered into a ship immediately; and that night *they caught nothing*." What a waste of precious time —not only of one man's but of seven! And if there is one thing more than another of which I am certain it is this, that their catching nothing was not for want of trying. It was not because they idled away the time or were lackadaisical in their project. There was not a lazy bone in Simon Peter or in any of his six companions. They *"toiled* all night". I can just picture how pleasantly bustling and officious Simon Peter would be as the managing director of the newly floated company, and how he would convince the other shareholders, even doubting Thomas, that the "net takings" would be a "big haul". But as the time wore on, the outlook became darker and darker. Just under the surface, there seemed to be a conspiracy of avoidance. All the possible customers kept well away, and there was simply "nothing doing"! As the grey dawn shimmered upon their tired bodies and disappointed minds, they were in very different mood from when they had jauntily sallied forth in the early watches of the night.

"That night they caught *nothing.*" That is always the outcome of self-directed service, so far as real, *spiritual* results are concerned. Very often, deeply spiritually-minded persons are impatiently misunderstood by others who are all for "*doing* something", simply because they discern spiritual values more truly than the less prayerful do. Sometimes, for instance, they are not quite so easily swept off their feet by enthusiasm for huge meetings which look glamorously successful to others; they detect the superficiality in the big excitement. At other times, perhaps, they perceive the hand of God and the moving of the Holy Spirit where others are discouraged by absence of "quick results". Oh, if we only prayed more! Oh, that more of us did spiritual work in a spiritual way! What well-meaning hurry and worry, what elaborate organisation and imposing-looking administration, go by the name of Christian service yet are largely prayerless and out of line with the will of Christ! It is not too easy to speak on these matters without being misunderstood, for in many connections, of course, there *has to be* organisation and administration. We are not blind to that, but our lament is that so much of *it* is blind, spiritually.

I have a dear friend in the Christian ministry, a man of outstanding gifts, who from the time of his conversion genuinely loved our Lord Jesus, and wanted to serve Him with all his capabilities. He determined to "get on" in the ministry, and he certainly *did* "get on"; for with such personality and pertinacity it could scarcely have been otherwise. He became the minister of a great church, from the pulpit of which he exerted a wide influence. There were all the appearances of success—numbers, members, prestige, popularity, replete treasury and expanding organisation. He was no mere individualist or isolationist either.

He championed the evangelical cause outside his own pulpit, and was highly rated by his ministerial brethren.

He was not given to outward boasting, nor, however, did he try to conceal from himself inwardly that he was a "special". In fact one morning, in his study, he inwardly said to himself, "I am like King Saul was in Israel, 'head and shoulders above his fellows' "; but even as he said it he was smitten in conscience, for he remembered that the same King Saul was also an utter failure as a theocratic shepherd-king of Israel, through his *self-will*. In one sudden flash my minister-friend saw his heart exposed, and there, right at the centre of all his busy ministry, was self-will and self-applauding pride. Right at the heart of his success was failure. He saw it, knew it, and was dazed by it. All his outward success now appeared as merely an empty shell. Moreover he now saw in an instant the explanation of something which had periodically exasperated him: although there had been aesthetic worship, decorous order, beaming politeness, as well as good, sound evangelical preaching in all his services, yet somehow, for some seemingly strange reason, the spiritual life of his church could never get beyond a certain point of "properness"; there was everything except the one really vital thing—everything but a living, spiritual *flame*!

That morning he saw as never before the spiritual *futility* of self-will service. Thank God, that morning also became the beginning of a new kind of serving, a serving henceforth Christ-directed and therefore Spirit-energised. He had formerly gone forth Peter-like, saying, "I go a fishing," but now, as never before, he saw the significance of our Master's word, "Follow Me, and *I will make you* fishers of men." Since that revealing, humbling, transforming hour, his service has become *vital*. What does he care about mere popularity any more? He has a fellowship with Christ, and a sense of spiritual direction, and a power to influence men for God, which he never knew before. Nor did he ever encounter such opposition from Satan before. Nor did he ever have such real spiritual success in the saving of souls and the leading of believers into "the fulness of blessing".

> Lord, how I long with eager mind
> Men's souls to save and bless!
> But yet, alas, how oft I find
> Much failure, small success!

In self-dictated haste to serve,
  With prayerless zeal I run;
Then weep with weary mind and nerve
  To find so little done.

Lord, clear my misted eyes to see
  That nothing can avail,
Until I learn, alone with Thee,
  Through praying to prevail.

What means my busy work to Thee,
  If done in vain self-will?
What power or guidance can there be,
  Till *Thou* Thy servant fill?

Lord, help me learn to wait until
  Thy will I clearly see;
Then fill me, guide me, and fulfil
  Thy perfect will through me.

"That night they caught nothing." How pathetically indeed do those seven men in that night-time fishing expedition show us the need of tarrying to ascertain the Master's will! Look back again over those four features of self-directed service. (1) It was in self-will—"I go a fishing". (2) It was under merely human leadership—"We also go with thee". (3) It was dangerously impulsive—"They entered into a ship immediately". (4) It was a disappointing failure—"That night they caught nothing".

Christ-directed Service

But now move on again to the surprise-ending of the episode. See the transformation from failure to success, all because self-directed service gave place to *Christ*-directed service. When the Lord becomes our Managing Director, the whole concern takes on a new aspect.

"But when the morning was now come, Jesus stood on the shore; though the disciples knew not that it was Jesus. Then Jesus saith unto them: Children, have ye any meat? They answered Him: No. And He said unto them: Cast the net on the right side of the ship, and ye shall find. They cast, therefore, and now they were not able to draw it for the multitude of fishes."

It seems that those seven companions of Jesus were within easy calling distance of the shore, yet did not recognise that familiar Figure, not even when that well-known, beloved voice rang out to them. Of course, they were tired, and maybe their eyes were duller than usual; or is it that you and I are meant to notice how service in self-will dims our eyes and ears to the presence and voice of our Master? Surely, they must have had *some* suspicion, however, as they obediently cast the net over the right side, strangely wondering at the prediction, "Ye shall find".

And as soon as they obeyed His direction, dragging failure gave place to abounding success. They perceived at once the operation of a superhuman power, and recognised their miracle-working Master—"It is the Lord!" Pick out quickly the four main features in this picture of Christ-directed service.

First, the toilers now had an *assurance* which they had hitherto lacked. When they now let down the net on the right side of the vessel, they knew that they were doing it simply at the direction of that lone Figure on the beach, and that He had assured them, *"Ye shall find"*. How nerving it is, in our service for Christ, to know that we are doing His specific bidding, and to have the assurance, therefore, that He will certainly crown it with success! That is the kind of assurance which gives us faith to try again even when it has seemed as though there was not a fish in the whole area.

Second, they now had a *success* which had eluded them before. The empty meshes became full. It was a case of "all hands on deck" for the happy emergency. Even so, our Lord Jesus can change *your* and *my* failures to success; and this applies to every part of our life and service for Him—home life, church life, work-day life, and whatever leisure remainder there may be. Perhaps some of us feel we cannot do much: but what we *can* do, we *ought* to do; and how can we best do it? We can best do it by prayerfully tarrying to seek His guidance and wisdom and endue-ment of "power from on high". He will make His will unmis-takeably clear if we give Him opportunity. Some unsaved soul, for instance, will be brought disturbingly into our thoughts; or some sick person whom we ought to visit; or some gift which we ought to make; or some spoken witness which we ought to give; or some letter which we ought to write; or some new venture in which we ought to engage; or some other Christian activity which we ought to undertake. This waiting on Christ to know His will really "works"; and oh, what time-waste, blundering, and failure it spares us in the end! Did not our Lord Himself say, "If any man willeth to do His will, *he shall know* . . ."? Yes, if we really wait to know His will, we shall *know* it; and then, in the doing of it, failure becomes success. Not that the success may always be on the outwardly big scale, or immediate, or spectacular, like that suddenly bulging fishing-net on Galilee. Success is not always *quite* like that—not in its *outward* appearances at least. But real success there will assuredly be, and we shall inwardly *know* that there is success, just as really as if it were statistically imposing.

Third, not only was there new assurance and new success, but there was also a new *recognition of Christ*. Suddenly, through the very transformation which He had effected, that mysterious Person on the shore was recognised. John exclaimed, "It is the Lord!" (verse 7). But all the others knew too (verse 12). It is always like that. When we are serving under self-management we lack a sense of His partnership with us; but when we are really doing *His* will, in *His* way, at *His* word, then, again and again, He makes His presence wonderfully clear, and near, and dear.

Many a group of church officebearers would do well to learn this lesson of failure turned to success, and blindness turned to a new recognition of Christ, through doing only His revealed will. Some time ago I heard about a Presbyterian church leader who was reading the year's report at the Annual Business Meeting. When it came to membership statistics he mournfully commented, "We have caught no new fish this year, but we have been kippering those which we already had"! Far too many churches nowadays are stuck at this "kippering" business. How many "churches" are wonderfully busy with non-stop rounds of religious activity which, so far as the will of Christ is concerned, are nothing more than gratuitous guess-work! Is it surprising that there is failure—failure in that which is really vital, failure in that spiritual, soul-regenerating mission which is the very *raison d'etre* of the organised church's existence? Oh the prayerless churches of our day! Oh, the proud, spiritual failure! Listen, ministers, elders, deacons, leaders, workers; the need is for prayer, **prayer, prayer,** and more prayer, to recapture a sense of divine direction, and to "hear what the Spirit saith unto the churches". It is *then* that we hear the voice from the shore, "Cast the net on the right side of the ship, and ye shall find." It is *then* that the net becomes full, and failure gives place to success. It is *then* that we make rapturous new discoveries of our Master's all-controlling presence, and find ourselves exclaiming, "It is the Lord!"

But, once again, that early-morning episode shows us that Christ-directed service is *Christ-sustained* service. As those long-ago disciples finished dragging that laden net to shore, they saw a fire kindled, "and fish laid thereon, and bread"; and a welcoming voice invited them, "Come and dine". It is ever so: our Lord says to all His servants who truly do His bidding, "Come and dine". He does not need anything that *we* can bring, for He has food already prepared (verse 9); yet He also says to us, "Bring of the fish which *ye* have now caught" (verse 10), sc that besides divine sustenance there may be human fellowship. Self-directed service is exhausting, not only physically and mentally, but spiritually, and is therefore wrong; but *Christ*-directed service brings these lovely replenishments on the shore. We are kept fresh, buoyant, gracious, kindly, and gladsome, instead of becoming impatient, downcast, irritable, and difficult to get on with. There is quiet retirement into His presence, for renewal through communion.

I think Peter never forgot that breakfast at yonder quiet spot by the lake that morning. He seems to allude to in Acts x. 40, 41, "Him God raised up the third day, and shewed Him openly; not to all the people, but unto witnesses chosen before of God, even to us, *who did eat and drink with Him after He rose from the dead.*" So is it with ourselves: some of those "Come and dine" experiences which we enjoy with our risen Lord after service according to His revealed will, are never-to-be-forgotten hours. The very joy of heaven takes possession of our hearts, and our joy no man taketh from us (John xvi. 22). How rich does prayer become at such times! How the Bible lights up with new inspiration! No reward could be dearer. Let our prayer ever be,

> Oh, use me, Lord, use even me
> Just as *Thou* wilt, and *when* and *where*;
> Until Thy blessed face I see,
> Thy rest, Thy joy, Thy glory share!

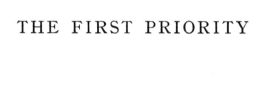

THE FIRST PRIORITY

Though I do not admire his ideas, I do admire the enthusiasm of that man Garibaldi. It is reported that when he marched towards Rome in 1867, they took him up and threw him into prison; and he wrote to his comrades, "If fifty Garibaldi's are thrown into prison, let Rome be free." That is the spirit. That is what we want in the cause of Christ. . . . A good many people are complaining all the time about themselves, and crying out, "My leanness, my leanness!" when they ought rather to say, "My laziness, my laziness!" . . . I believe in what John Wesley used to say, "All at it, and always at it."

D. L. Moody.

THE FIRST PRIORITY

"Ye shall receive power after that the Holy Spirit is come upon you; and ye shall be witnesses unto Me, both in Jerusalem and in all Judaea, and in Samaria, and unto the uttermost part of the earth."—Acts i. 8.

WE ARE speaking to those who have "obtained like precious faith with us in the righteousness of our God and Saviour Jesus Christ" (2 Pet. i. 1, R.V.); to those who know

> The inward calm of sins forgiven,
> Of peace with God and hope of heaven.

Of all concerns and privileges the greatest and highest is that of knowing and possessing the Son of God as our Saviour. The more we contemplate it, the more wonderful it becomes, and the more we long to serve Him "whom having not seen (as yet) we love" (1 Pet. i. 8).

There are three things which every would-be servant of the Lord Jesus should firmly grasp: (1) The first priority in service is soul-winning. (2) The mightiest weapon in service is prayer. (3) The ruling motive in service must be love. Just here we are to think only about the first of these, namely, soul-winning.

Let us settle it in our minds once for all that our Lord means soul-winning to be the "first priority" in our service for Him. Many believers are in error concerning this. They fall into the common mistake of thinking that Christian service is some form of activity in meetings or societies inside a church, or at least in connection with some religious organisation. They suppose that it mainly consists in preaching or testifying in meetings, or being a secretary or treasurer or committee-member or some other kind of helper in a religious association of some kind. The spare time of many a Christian is almost wholly absorbed by such things. Yet when we thoughtfully review the matter, what is it,

173

in strict truth and above all else, which we all long to do for the Saviour? It is to win souls to Him, or at least to influence them toward Him. The foremost aim and most vital form of Christian service is witness-bearing for the Saviour, with a view to the salvation of the unsaved.

This, of course, may usefully *include* the persuading of people to attend churches or meetings. Sound, evangelical churches and movements are strategic points to which unconverted persons may be prayerfully and honourably *lured*. Such canvassing is real service; and many Christians are at fault in neglecting it. There is an obvious place and need for good, sound, evangelical churches and organisations; but the thing which we are intensely concerned to emphasise here is the rather startling fact that for the majority of us the most urgent form of Christian service lies *outside* these; and it is this simply vital work of witness-bearing to the unsaved, or (as it is often called) *individual evangelism*. The over-plentiful indoor meetings and organisations of today, good as they may be in themselves, become even a *bane* when they so occupy us that individual soul-winning is crowded out.

It is easy to forget the end in the means, and to think that because all the organisational machinery is running busily a lot is being accomplished. But there can be a great deal of religious activity which is little more than going round in a circle and not getting any further in things vital. Dear fellow-believer, let us be convinced: this one-by-one endeavour to lead souls into saving union with the Saviour is our *first-important* service.

With this in mind, think again of our Master's words just before He bodily and visibly ascended to heaven, never to be seen again on earth until His still-future second advent:

"YE SHALL RECEIVE POWER AFTER THAT THE HOLY SPIRIT IS COME UPON YOU; AND YE SHALL BE WITNESSES UNTO ME, BOTH IN JERUSALEM AND IN ALL JUDAEA, AND IN SAMARIA, AND UNTO THE UTTERMOST PART OF THE EARTH."

If I were wanting to open up this text in a strictly homiletical way, I should say that the subject of it is Christian witnessing, and that there are three notable features indicated: (1) Christ is the *focus*—"Ye shall be witnesses unto Me"; (2) the world is the *scope*—"Jerusalem . . . the uttermost part of the earth"; (3) the

Holy Spirit is the *power*—"Ye shall receive power after that the Holy Spirit is come upon you".

Just here, however, it may be advantageous to disregard homiletical rigidity, and allow the stream of our thoughts to make its own free channel, in and around the words.

To us Spirit-born believers, who comprise the true Church, God has given the greatest mission in the world, and the greatest message in the world, and the greatest Master in the world. Our mission is to *save* men. Our message is the *Gospel*. Our Master is the *risen Christ*. Never was there more urgent reason than today for us to fulfil our divine mission. Never was there more pressing need than today for us to proclaim our divine message. Never was there more clamant challenge than today for us to obey the great commission of our divine Master.

Winds of evil have heaved their foul breath over the earth. Ambitious despots have usurped dictatorship over millions of our fellow-creatures; and millions more are imperilled. Bad politics curse the nations, and false cults jeopardise Christendom. The call of the hour to Protestant churches is to break free from the parasite entanglements of secondary issues and less-important absorptions which sap their strength and foil their progress, and to get back to the unrecinded, original mandate in its august simplicity:

"YE SHALL RECEIVE POWER AFTER THAT THE HOLY SPIRIT IS COME UPON YOU; AND YE SHALL BE WITNESSES UNTO ME, BOTH IN JERUSALEM AND IN ALL JUDAEA, AND IN SAMARIA, AND UNTO THE UTTERMOST PART OF THE EARTH."

Why, that is how the whole, wonderful story of the historic Church began: Christ went up; the Spirit came down; the disciples went out. Are we reaching out today with the old-time vision? Are we witnessing today with the old-time success? Are we experiencing today the old-time power? The New Testament ideal is: every individual Christian a soul-winner, and every local church an evangelising centre; but in most instances we are far removed from that today! In view of the vast and ominous international developments of our times, we are needing, more than ever, a new invasion of the Holy Spirit, a new immersion in the compassions of Christ, and a new revival of individual soul-winning. Each one of us will do well to recall again the sound words of dear old Richard Baxter: "I cannot do everything, but I can do something. What I *can* do, I *ought* to do; and what I *ought* to do, by the grace of God I *will* do."

Make me a winner of souls, Lord,
Teach me the art, I pray.
Show me, dear Master, Thy secret,
Whisper the words to say.
Give me Thy Spirit's anointing,
Use me, O Lord, each day.

Make me a winner of souls, Lord,
Let me Thy partnership prove.
Give me Thine hourly direction,
Wisdom that comes from above.
Tutor me, Lord, in Thy patience,
Pour through my lips Thy love.

What Soul-winning Is

Let us remember that in all our witnessing Christ must be the focus. We are not trying merely to make people religious. We are not trying to make Baptists, or Methodists, or Congregationalists, or Episcopalians, or denominationalists of any other kind. Much as we abhor the pseudo-church of Rome and its cruelly oppressive hierarchy, we are not trying even to make people Protestants. We are seeking to bring men and women, youths and young women, boys and girls, into regenerating union with the Son of God Himself, as their personal Saviour, whether by nominal connection they are Romanist, Protestant, Anglican, Nonconformist, or anything else. All merely denominational aspects must be viewed as severely subsidiary to this bringing of human beings into saving relationship with Christ.

Even apart from the eternal issues involved in this, we cannot do a more *patriotic* thing than seek to bring our fellow-nationals into this revolutionising experience of our Lord's saviourhood. Some time ago, I heard of an amusing incident in a British railway train. In one of the compartments there were just three occupants—a gentleman trying to read a book, a middle-aged woman, and an obstreperous young boy who simply would not stop talking nor sit still. The gentleman sat in a corner, trying to read his book. The woman and her unruly junior were at the far corner on the opposite side. The book-reader did his best to concentrate; the boy did his best to distract him; while the mother did her best to maintain respect for the one and restraint over the other. They were all doing their best in one way or another, but it precipitated a major disaster. The would-be reader kept looking up at the interrupting youngster. The mother kept up a running commentary of "Sit still!" and "Be quiet!"; until, all her powers of non-violent subjugation being exhausted, she seized the cantankerous young rascal, laid him over her knee, and soundly spanked him. At this, the outraged bookman started up, took off his spectacles, and with a look of intellectual agony in his eyes exclaimed, "Oh, madam, have you not heard about the new methods of psychology?" The woman replied, "Yes, sir, I'se heerd all about that; but *this is quicker*"!

Yes, "this is quicker"!—and by a sharp rebound from the humorous to the intensely serious, we claim that this one-by-one plan of winning souls to the Saviour is a quicker way of social betterment than any other. In these days of disturbingly increased juvenile and adolescent criminality, various counter-measures such as clubs, societies, sports groups, camps, classes, are advocated by anxious leaders. We have nothing but goodwill for all such well-conducted activities; but if our leaders will believe it, the quickest and surest way to transform human character is by conversion to Christ. When a man becomes truly converted to Christ, he becomes a better husband, a better father, a better workman, a better citizen, a better all-round man. The same is true of any woman, of any boy, of any girl. To those who complain that the one-by-one method seems "so slow", we reply that it is only slow because so few are doing it. If there were a large-scale rededication to this business of individual evangelism, what mighty changes might be wrought!

Present-day Difficulties

We may as well face up to this, however, that soul-winning is made the more difficult today by reason of certain disadvantageous developments which are upon us.

Foremost among these is *the changed attitude to the Bible*. Until a couple of generations ago, even among the irreligious, in Britain and America, the Bible was acknowledged to have a unique authority, and was accorded a corresponding respect; but today this veneration has been largely broken down among the masses, due to theological radicalism, so that now, in many cases, a quotation from the Bible carries little or no more weight than a quotation from Shakespeare, or even H. G. Wells. So long as the Bible was regarded as authoritative, the soul-winner's task was comparatively straightforward; but the changed attitude of today toward the Bible greatly "queers the pitch", and adds complexity to the soul-winner's task.

Then, again, going with this changed attitude to the Bible is an appallingly increased *ignorance of the Bible*. Formerly, in Britain and America there was a background of elementary Christian knowledge in most people's minds, to which evangelists and Christian workers could make an intelligible appeal; but many of our younger and middle-aged people of today know scarcely anything of this; and certainly such ignorance is a great set-back to soul-winning.

Yet again, there is no doubt that soul-winning is made more difficult today by *the misleading nature of much modern religion*. Organised Christianity today is marked by a decline in the teaching of evangelical doctrine, and a recrudescence of ritualism. The breakdown in Biblical indoctrination is an outcome of that ultra-critical theological radicalism commonly called "Modernism". The reversion to ritual is a clerical endeavour to fill the gap created by the decline of doctrinal teaching; but it is a deceptive and futile substitute. It is like putting an elaborately-dressed-up corpse in the place of a living organism. It is the attempt to conceal inward death by outward show. It is like setting the dinner-table with ornate crockery and cutlery, but serving nothing to eat. It is the mere symbol instead of the substance; empty ritual instead of solid reality. Doctrine, the teaching of the truth, is that by which men learn and live; and no amount of ritual can make up for its absence. "A living dog is better than a dead lion," and a spiritually-alive mission hall is far more than a dead cathedral. The breakdown in doctrine is pathetic in the British Nonconformist bodies; and the increase in ritual is glaring in the English State Church. Because of this, the rank and file of the people are left in obscurity as to what the distinctive message of the Church and its ministers really is. People are not to be blamed if they judge Christianity by the churches and the ministers. This creates an added problem for the true soul-winner; for in many instances, before the real truth of the Gospel can be got into a human heart, there has to be a counteracting of the errors by which it has been deceived in much that passes as Christianity today. How many of us, after struggling to win a soul, have had to come back sighing with Nehemiah, "There is much rubbish so that we are not able to build the wall"! (Neh. iv. 10.)

Then, once more, soul-winning is made the more difficult today by *the multitude of distractions* which beset men and women. This is a day of multiplied amusements, on the one hand, and multiplied anxieties on the other. Youth is mesmerised by multiplied worldly amusements and earthly ambitions, while maturer life is put to strain by the pressure of problems and anxieties inherent in our restless, complicated way of living, and the tense uncertainty of international relationships, and the worry of children who, having been brought up under the unhealthy spell of the "new psychology" and television, refuse many of the healthy restraints which conditioned life in the days of their parents. With increased gaiety on the one hand, and increased gravity on the other, people's minds are more distractingly preoccupied with worldly concerns today than ever formerly. There is such pressure in many lives today that there is scarcely the heart to concentrate on so-called "religious" matters. All this makes the task of winning souls for Christ more difficult.

The One Great Provision

We are not unmindful that besides peculiar difficulties, there are unique opportunities today—and may we seize them! What we are here stressing is that be the obstacles what they may, this vital activity of winning souls must go on: it is our Master's most sacred trust to all His followers throughout this present age.

Does not *He* know and understand the problems we are up against today? From the slopes of Olivet did He not pre-delineate the whole course of these two A.D. centuries? Yes, He foreknew all; and He anticipatively covered the whole of it by one, all-sufficient provision: *"YE SHALL RECEIVE POWER AFTER THAT THE HOLY SPIRIT IS COME UPON YOU."*

Those first disciples certainly *did* "receive power" when the Holy Spirit had "come upon" *them,* and they "turned the world upside down". He has come upon millions of others *since* then, transforming their weakness into power, and making them "mighty through God to the pulling down of strongholds" (2 Cor. x. 4). But where is the manifestation of that power today? It is the exception, and not the rule. There is much eagerness to serve; but what is more pathetic than powerless eagerness?

In our Protestant churches of today the generality of our people are taught nothing at all about the enduement of "power from on high" (Luke xxiv. 49). And even those who read daily portions of the New Testament for themselves seem to expect no more than the standard set by the poverty-stricken pulpit. Here and there, like lovely oases in a wide-spreading desert, one finds exceptions, but oh, the spiritual Sahara of modern Protestantism! Romanism, Communism, and heterodox cults make headway mainly because of the spiritual sterility and inertia of the Protestant denominations. There is a famine in Canaan, and the people go down into Egypt (Gen. xii. 10). The brook which refreshed God's mighty Elijahs is dried up (1 Kings xvii. 7). The most devastating blight on modern Protestantism is its chaotic uncertainty about the Bible. Samson is shorn of his locks. The Delilah of a pseudo-Biblical scholarship has beguiled and betrayed him. His eyes are put out, and he grinds for the Philistines.

Protestant Christianity will never regain the initiative until there is a return to faith in a supernaturally inspired and authoritative Bible. Meanwhile, the experience of "enduement" by the Holy Spirit remains something entirely outside the cognisance of the average church member.

Even among the evangelically sound churches, the teaching and experiencing of this enduement is far from usual. The evangelical churches have been so embroiled in the intellectual struggle against theological liberalism that some of the deeper spiritual emphases have been crushed out. Then again, the whole tenor of the times, the tense hurry of modern life, and the congestion of our twentieth-century urbanised civilization, are heavily against the habit of unhurried, secret waiting upon God for the receiving of this promised filling by the Spirit.

Our Lord's word to the first disciples was, *"Tarry ye* in the

city of Jerusalem until ye be endued with power from on high."
In one sense there seems no need for any such tarrying today,
for the fullness of the Spirit, once-for-all given at Pentecost, is still
with us, in abiding and immediate availability. Yet there is
another sense in which we *do* need to "tarry". As soon as ever
we begin to wait on God with serious resolve to "obtain the blessing", we become aware of our disqualifying unpreparedness.
There cannot be this "enduement" of the "power from on high"
until there is utter dedication to Christ, and sanctification of the
heart. Thus we find the need to "tarry until . . ."

But, oh, the blessing is real; and where there is sincere yielding
of heart to Christ, the tarrying need not be a long-drawn-out
waiting. In this connection, those who really "wait *on* the Lord"
do not have long to wait "*for* Him". His willingness to bestow
always matches our preparedness to receive.

We are not all "endued" to become Luthers or Calvins or
Whitefields or Spurgeons or great public champions of "the faith
once-for-all delivered to the saints"; but all of us who tarry
until we receive the blessing are endued as our Master's *witnesses*.
"Ye shall be *witnesses unto Me*." Nor are we all endued so as
to "speak with tongues", or to "heal the sick" or to be "workers
of miracles". Far oftener, one of the first and most reliable
evidences of the Spirit's infilling is that we learn to hold the one
tongue which we already have! But when we *do* speak under
the enduement of the Spirit, our words have a wisdom and a
worth and a weight which only He can give.

Yes, we are "endued" to be our Lord's *witnesses*; and each
one of us has a constituency of friends and relatives, workmates
and associates in which our individual witness has, or *can* have,
peculiar influence. Many of us have grown discouraged because
of little or no apparent results, and have decided that we can do
no more than just try to "live the life" of a Christian before
them, and leave the speaking part to others. Deep down in our
hearts we are disturbed and sad about it; but what can we do?

I will tell you what we can do. We can tell the Lord again
that we love Him, and long to be used by Him in our sphere of
influence. We can resolve to get alone with Him, and wait upon
Him until this enduement of "power from on high" comes upon
us. We need not fear that the experience will make us religious

oddities. It will restore to us the lovely naturalness of the perfect humanhood revealed in Jesus. It will give us a deep and satisfying consciousness of our Lord's indwelling, and of His love toward us. It will be both *con*straining and *re*straining. It will be "mouth, matter, and wisdom". It will not convert everyone to whom we bear witness, for as it was with our Lord Himself, and with the protomartyr Stephen, so is it still today: men may resist our *witness* even when they cannot refute our *wisdom*. But there will be a telling-power in our witnessing which was never there before, and many *will* be drawn to the Saviour through our words.

This enduement of "power from on high" is the secret of transformation from dumbness and defeat to testimony with telling-power. If it were to become experienced on a considerable scale again, it would prove the golden key to evangelical revival; for, after all, the most convincing apologetic of the evangelical faith and message is the "*demonstration* of the Spirit and power" (1 Cor. ii. 4) in it and through it. Lord, stir us to renewed and persevering prayer! Lord, increase our compassions for the perishing! Lord, endue us with the "power from on high"! Lord, make us Thine effective witnesses! Lord, use us in the saving of souls!

The Threefold Challenge

Finally, let us reflect again on the fact that this winning of souls to Christ is undoubtedly the *supreme* service of the Christian. There are three aspects of this which should ever be in our minds.

First, it *fulfils the highest of all functions to our fellow-creatures.* The highest service we can ever render to another human being is to help him, or her, into saving union with the Son of God. Perhaps it is understandable that some among us who feel deficient in natural gifts, or seem frustrated by disadvantageous circumstances, should sometimes long for that ampler life in the heavenly realm where we shall be able to render such service as is impossible at present. In that fuller existence we shall have sinless hearts and perfected powers, increased capacities and enlarged capabilities. We may be endowed with faculties and senses to which we are oblivious here on earth. "Eye hath not seen, nor ear heard, neither have entered into the heart of man, the things which God hath prepared for them that love Him." In that land which is fairer than day, we may vie with cherubs and seraphs in swift-winged prosecution of our King's bidding. As we sometimes sing,

> Then we shall be what we should be,
> And we will be what we would be;
> Things that are not now, nor could be,
> Then shall be our own.

Yet it is salutary to bear this fact in mind, that whatever opportunities or superiorities may be ours in yonder higher life, the greatest of all service which we can *ever* do is that which we are called to do here and now, in this present short life, namely, the winning of souls to a vital faith in the Son of God, and thereby bringing about their eternal salvation. I repeat it: no service which we can ever do in heaven can possibly be greater than *that*. The solemn words with which James closes his epistle make it abundantly clear: "Let him know, that he which converteth the sinner from the error of his way shall save a soul from death, and shall hide a multitude of sins" (Jas. v. 20). Think what it means to save a soul from "the wrath to come", from the judgment of the "Great White Throne", from the "outer darkness", the "lake of fire", and the "second death"; to save it to regeneration and sanctification and eternal glorification! Some time ago, in a Canadian magazine, I noticed the following report of an utterance by an atheist: —

"Did I firmly believe, as millions say they do, that the knowledge and practice of religion in this life influences destiny in another, religion would mean to me everything. I should cast away earthly enjoyments as dross, earthly cares as follies, and earthly thoughts and feelings as vanity. Religion would be my first thought on waking, and my last image before sleep sank me into unconsciousness. I should labour in its cause alone. I should take thought for the morrow of eternity alone. I should esteem one soul gained for heaven worth a life of suffering. Earthly consequences should never stay my hand or seal my lips. Earth, its joys and its griefs, should occupy no moment of my thoughts. I should strive to look upon eternity alone, and on the immortal souls around me, soon to be everlastingly happy or everlastingly miserable. I should go forth to the world and preach to it in season and out of season, and my text would be, 'What shall it profit a man if he gain the whole world and lose his soul?'"

What a rebuke do that atheist's words carry for many of us! It was with the same vivid sense of the unutterable issues at stake that the saintly Brainerd wrote: "I cared not where or how I lived, or what hardships I went through, so that I could gain souls to Christ." Truly, to win a soul to Christ fulfils the highest of all functions! God make us wise to win souls while the day of present opportunity lingers!

Second, the winning of souls to Christ *obeys the last and most sacred of all our Lord's commands.* How carefully we cherish the parting words of our now-departed loved-ones, or of notable leaders! How often people have said to me, "You see, I keep on doing this thing because it was my own dear mother's parting wish"; or, "I can never forget it, for it was my father's last request to me before he passed over"! Well, this is the last word of Jesus, just before His visible, bodily ascension to heaven:

"YE SHALL RECEIVE POWER, AFTER THAT THE HOLY SPIRIT IS COME UPON YOU: AND YE SHALL BE WITNESSES UNTO ME BOTH IN JERUSALEM, AND IN ALL JUDAEA, AND IN SAMARIA, AND UNTO THE UTTERMOST PART OF THE EARTH."

Have you ever tried to picture the scene in heaven when Jesus ascended there in that glory-cloud of long ago? What a welcome there would be as the angels thronged around to make a shining guard of honour for the beloved Victor! Someone has supposed that soon after the ascension the following conversation took place between the Lord Jesus and the angel Gabriel.

GABRIEL: "Master, you died for the whole world down there, did you not?"
JESUS: "Yes."
GABRIEL: "You must have suffered much" (with an earnest look into the wonderful but scarred face).
JESUS: "Yes."
GABRIEL: "And do they all know about it?"
JESUS: "Oh, no; only a few people in Palestine know about it, so far."
GABRIEL: "Well, Master, what is your plan? What has been done about telling the world that you have died and provided redemption?"
JESUS: "I asked Peter, and James, and John, and Andrew, and some others of them down there, to make it the business of their lives to tell others; and the others are to tell others, and the others still others, until the last man in the farthest circle has heard."

GABRIEL: (Who feels doubt about the plan after contacts with us folk down here) "Yes . . . but . . . suppose Peter fails? . . . Suppose that after a time John fails? . . . and suppose they do *not* tell others? Or suppose that those who come afterward fail to keep on telling others. . . . What then?"

JESUS: (With eyes full of tenderness and longing) "Gabriel, I haven't made any other plan. *I'm counting on them.*"

That is the very truth: He is *counting on you and me.* He indicated so, in His last command; and for the Christian, that parting command should outrank all other loyalties.

Third, the winning of souls *receives the highest of all rewards.* Who among us has not halted again and again at Daniel xii. 3, "And they that be wise shall shine as the brightness of the firmament, and they that turn many to righteousness as the stars for ever and ever"? Well, let us (so to speak) New Testamentise it: "They that be witnesses to the saving power of the Gospel . . . and they that win souls for Christ shall shine as the stars for ever." If even a "cup of cold water" given in the Master's name shall in no wise lose its reward, what shall the reward be of those who have brought many living gems to the Saviour's feet? Mrs. Cousins has put into poetic form what the saintly soul-winner, Samuel Rutherford, wrote from his prison cell to his parishioners in Anwoth, Scotland.

> Fair Anwoth by the Solway,
> To me thou still art dear.
> E'en from the verge of heaven
> I spill for thee a tear.
> Oh, if one soul from Anwoth
> Meet me at God's right hand,
> My heaven will be ten heavens,
> In Emmanuel's land.

Yes, to see others there in that pure glory and sinless rapture, whom we have led to the Saviour, must surely make heaven "ten heavens" to us! What simply unimaginable reward flashes out from those words, "as the stars, for ever and ever"! The society "stars" and movie "stars" of this present glamorous but evil and remorseless world—how soon their fickle dazzle is quenched in everlasting night! But *God's* "stars" shine on and on through unending heaven! Oh, to be an ambitious soulwinner!—for *that* ambition humbles and purifies as it exalts and glorifies. Oh, to be able to say with Paul: "Though I be free from all men, yet have I made myself servant unto all that I might gain the more. . . . I am made all things to all men, that I might by all means save some" (1 Cor. ix. 19, 22)!

Dear Christian, whom I now address, what about *your* going "from house to house" as Paul did? What about *your* going out to help with the open-air witness? What about *your* giving out carefully selected tracts to the unsaved? What about *your* talking to friends and workmates concerning Christ, as discreet opportunism suggests? What about writing those letters which might be like very arrows from the quiver of the Almighty, or like balm of Gilead from the heavenly Physician? What about *your* seizing opportunities in cars and trains and buses and in casual contacts? Yes, of course, there will be rebuffs (though much depends on the way one says and does things), and sometimes we may be made to feel small (though never *too* small!), and sometimes we may feel that not much has been accomplished (though often at such times our words are most of all having unsuspected effect). Once again we say it, and emphasise it: this witness-bearing for our Saviour and Master, this soul-saving work of bringing others to Him, is the *supreme* service to which we can give ourselves. With a new sense of wonder at our own salvation, and a new sense of urgency as we mingle among the unconverted all around us, let us here and now rededicate ourselves to this highest of all endeavours.

> Make me a winner of souls, Lord,
>   Little my time seems free;
> Daily employment absorbs it,
>   Openings seem rare to me.
> Help me to gather time's fragments,
>   These would I use for Thee.
>
> Make me a winner of souls, Lord,
>   Brave against Satan's frown.
> Give me the grace of endurance,
>   Even tho' sometimes cast down.
> Ever my dearest ambition—
>   Gems for my Saviour's crown.

PRAYER IS SERVICE

One reason why we do not have more answers to our prayers is that we are not thankful enough. The divine injunction is, "Be careful for nothing, but in everything by prayer and supplication *with thanksgiving* let your requests be made known unto God." Someone has well said that there are three things in that verse—careful for nothing, prayerful for everything, thankful for anything.

Faith says, "Amen" to everything that God says. Faith takes God without any ifs. If God says it, faith answers, "Amen; I believe it."

D. L. Moody.

PRAYER IS SERVICE

"Pray without ceasing."—I Thess. v. 17.
"Brethren, pray for us."—I Thess. v. 25.

NEVER can we be reminded too often that Christians are "saved to serve"—saved to save others. Nor can it be too often added that our greatest weapon in Christian service is *prayer*, for most of us seem afflicted with a chronic forgetfulness of this.

There need be no envy or jealousy among the Lord's servants, for our personalities are so varied that each one of us can serve Him in a way which is distinctively different from all others. In any case the outward *form* of service is a quite secondary value. The supreme fact and glory of Christian service is, that *whichever* visible form it assumes, it is service for *HIM*. If two of the heavenly seraphs were sent down to this world, one to be a high-ranking leader, the other to be a street-sweeper, do you think there would be any quarrel as to which role each should fill? The great thing to *their* minds would be that in either case the service was for *HIM*. Despite the outward disparity of form and earthly rank, the real, inward dignity and privilege would be equal. Indeed, if the two seraphs were to indulge any preference at all, I think it would be in favour of the street-sweeping, as giving more opportunity to express utter love, humility, and adoration toward their glorious King.

See that stately, liturgical service in the majestic cathedral. Then, peep into that noisy, stuffy slum-mission where an ungowned, plain-dressed worker is kneeling at the penitent-rail with a ragged, returning prodigal. In the eyes of heaven, there may be far more *real* dignity about that mission hall than about the cathedral.

Even the more spiritually minded among us are continually prone to the subtle fault of estimating service values in terms of outward levels and natural gifts. If a man has fine physique, handsome features, prepossessing personality, sonorous voice, captivating felicity of utterance, and he consecrates all these to public Christian ministry, he is obviously the right man in the right place; but let not his brethren who are devoid of such public accomplishments fall into the discouraging snare of thinking that he can therefore render *truer* service to Christ than *they*. A great deal of widely public and outwardly impressive Christian ministry has far less *real* service for Christ in it than the unobtrusive, unnoticed, patient, prayerful, plodding struggle of a Sunday School teacher with a class of obstreperous boys, in an out-of-the-way Sunday School.

Many who have made the biggest noise "down here" will be little heard of "up there"; and many who have had no public gifts on earth will have much public reward in heaven. That which our Lord watches most of all in His servants is *motive*. That which He prizes most of all is love to Himself, sincerity, prayerfulness. Let not those who are without the more popular, public gifts envy those who have them, for they are a heavy responsibility; and those to whom much has been given, by way of natural talent, of them will much be required. Let not those whose service must be rendered in the background be jealous of those who serve in the forefront, for public Christian service is beset by wilier temptations and deadlier perils than any other. Every public servant of the Lord is a special target of the devil.

Moreover, all present, earthly distinctions of social stratum and natural gift are merely temporary. They are not the basic things. The basic thing is motive. *All* service, however insignificant it may seem when judged by worldly standards, if it springs from true love to Christ is "great in the sight of the Lord" (Luke i. 15); for "man looketh on the outward appearance, but the Lord looketh on the heart" (1 Sam. xvi. 7).

Meanwhile, each one of us is just as God permitted and situated, in His overruling purpose. Therefore, let none of us envy another. We are all equally yet distinctively dear to the Son of God our Saviour. The same precious blood which was shed for John and Peter and Paul was shed for you and me. You and I were equally costly to redeem as they, and are equally dear to the heart which was broken for us. Gifts are secondary. Love is everything. Each of us is accountable. Each of us has opportunity to serve, and we only think otherwise when our faculty of inward vision is diseased. I believe that God has a special work for each one of us, and that if we fail to do it, then it will not be done by any other. I did not always believe this, for the universe is very big, and we are physically infinitesimal; but after careful consideration I have come to hold it most definitely as a very precious article of belief. Dear fellow-Christian, I believe this:

> There's a work for Jesus,
>   Ready at your hand;
> 'Tis a task the Master
>   Just for you has planned.
> Haste to do His bidding;
>   Yield Him service true.
> There's a work for Jesus,
>   None but *you* can do!

Christian, whom I now address, do not you yourself believe the same? Deep down in your heart, do you not feel and know it to be true? Does not the Written Word teach it? Does not the inward witness of the Spirit confirm it? Does not the testimony of other believers endorse it? If the scope of this present address permitted, we could give instance after instance of dear saints who thought that illness or other adverse circumstances had completely cut them off from Christian service, and then discovered that their imaginary prison-bars were in reality a golden gateway to new and lovelier service for their King. Yes, "there's a work for Jesus, none but *you* can do"!

Prayer Is the Greatest

And now, after venting these preliminary reflections, I come back to this, that the greatest *instrument* of service is prayer. I do not say that prayer is the *only* service, for there are many other forms and ways; but it is the greatest, and indeed is basic to all others. We can do much more than pray, *after* we have prayed; but we cannot do *more* than pray *until* we have prayed. We are never further ahead spiritually than we are in prayer.

Now it may be that certain believers whom we here address have the perplexity of longing to serve the Lord Jesus but not knowing just what to do, or how or where to begin. In that case we call attention to the following fact: In the providence of God, *the greatest of all possible service is something that any of us can do, whoever or whatever or wherever we are.* There are many ways of serving Christ to the good of our fellow-men; but the *GREATEST* way of serving is one which lies open to *ALL*; and it is the ministry of *prayer.*

Yes, after some hesitation and much pondering, I believe that prayer is the greatest of all service. It is the mightiest weapon of the Church, and the highest ministry of the individual believer. Perhaps the most ironic tragedy of modern evangelical Christianity is that its most powerful spiritual apparatus is the most neglected. In many churches (so-called) the prayer meeting has become quite defunct. In others, attendances have dwindled to a mere handful of the elderly. Ideally, the prayer meeting is the congregational appointment with God; but actually how often it is crowded out by a committee meeting, or even by some giddy operetta! Oh, this God-dishonouring sin of the churches! Is it to be wondered at that so many of them make a sorry spectacle of impotency? The fatal fault is lack of prayer.

The very *lack* of it today accentuates the *need* for it; and I would say to all those believers who are longing to render effective service for Christ: Give yourselves to the ministry of prayer; for besides excelling all other forms of service, it is open to all, even the least gifted.

But *why* is prayer the greatest of all service? Well, for one thing it has *the fewest limitations.* Take any other form of service, and observe the limitations which beset it. In *preaching,* for example, there is limitation of space in which one can be heard; limitation of locality in the sense that one can be in only one place at a time; limitation of bodily strength, voice, lung-power, not to mention hostile prejudices, or limitations of personality-appeal. Even though radio and television have widened some of these limitations, they have not eliminated them.

It is the same with *writing.* The printed page can do what the speaking voice cannot. It lasts much longer, and sometimes lives on for generations. Yet how many are its limitations! Besides cost of production which is prohibitive to many of us, there is severe limitation in possibility of circulation, even if we could always write "best sellers"; limitation through diversity of languages, even if we ourselves as the authors could write in several; limitation through illiteracy, antipathy, disinclination for reading. So is it with other kinds of service.

But with *prayer* it is different. It is free from all such limitations. As a kind of spiritual radio it makes its way directly into the hearts of those for whom we pray. It quietly passes through walls and locked doors, gets into prisons and palaces, into slums and mansions, takes hold of rich and poor, high and low, learned and unlearned, old and young, and demonstrates its omnipresent limitlessness in a thousand ways.

Then, again, prayer is the greatest of all service because most of all it brings *God* into the picture. Some time ago, a well-known Christian leader was walking along a city street when he became attracted by a couple of boys who were peering with obvious wonder at some object inside a shop window. On pausing, he found that they were watching a large revolving globe-map of the earth, over which were the words, "HOLD UP YOUR HAND, AND SEE THE WORLD GO ROUND." Between the globe and the window pane was a transparent disc which caused the globe slowly to revolve when a hand was pressed against the window. It was this which held the rapt attention of the boys; and my friend confessed that in a minute or two he himself had fallen under its spell. There was a strange fascination, he said, in holding up one's hand, and then seeing the world begin to move round! And have we never heard the saying, "Prayer moves the Hand that moves the world"? It is true. Prayer enlists the omnipotence, omniscience, and omnipresence of *GOD*.

A while before the Second World War, I was in conversation with one of the leading officials of a large missionary society, when he related to me the following incident. A missionary and his wife, with ten stations under their charge, had appealed for ten spiritually-minded prayer-partners in the home country to cover those ten stations with intensive daily prayer. Up to the time of which I am now speaking, the missionary headquarters in England had secured only seven of the required ten intercessors. These seven had faithfully continued in daily intercession, crying urgently to God for victory and blessing on each of the seven stations which they respectively represented. After a few months of this, a letter came from the missionary and his wife, saying that something had happened which had greatly gladdened them, yet at the same time had puzzled them. A wonderful work of conversion and revival had broken out in seven of their stations, while the remaining three continued as hard and unresponsive as ever! The explanation was clear. "Prayer changes things." "More things are wrought by prayer than this world dreams of." Prayer in the name of Jesus and under the compulsion of the Holy Spirit accomplishes what all else is unable to do. I believe that if our overseas missionaries as a whole were asked to sum up in one verse of Scripture what they most of all beg that we at home should do for them, they would seize on 1 Thessalonians v. 25: "Brethren, *PRAY* for us."

Oh, this omnipresent potency of prayer! With such a means of service in our hands, is not prayerlessness a form of *sin*? Was it not with a prophet's insight that Samuel said, "God forbid that I should sin against the Lord in ceasing to pray for you" (1 Sam. xii. 23)? I may not be called to go to China or Africa or India as an overseas missionary, but I may really operate there through this mysterious but mighty agency of prayer! I thereby become independent of bodily and geographical limitations. True prayer is a projecting of one's personality into the invisible realm, and an allying of the will with that of our Lord against the powers of evil. In His absolute omnipotence, God, the Creator of all, could instantaneously blast all the enemies of light into utter oblivion, if He so willed; but that would be no *moral* victory for God; indeed, it would *frustrate* the moral victory which God is seeking, before the watching eyes of His universe, through the *loving* and *voluntary* co-operation of the redeemed in Christ. If only all Christian believers might grasp this, how it would transform their praying! How vital and strategic and compelling would prayer become to them!

A widely used servant of God tells how one Sunday evening, at a time when he had wandered far from God, he was arrested by a vibrant message which came over the radio. Evensong was being broadcast from an Anglican church. There was a virility in the preacher's voice, in contrast with the all-too-often sing-song style; and there was something magnetic in the message, the subject of which was the power of prayer. The speaker maintained that it was a duty resting upon all of us to pray for our friends. To make a habit of this might impose considerable demands upon time and memory, but it was not merely worthwhile, it was of transcendent importance. Of course, so the speaker went on, if one had only a few friends it would not take much time; but if some of his hearers were among the lucky ones with more friends than they could remember all at once, then the thing to do would be to index them, and pray for them by instalments. Then the preacher added, *"We don't know what we may be doing, if we pray for a friend tonight."*

I think that those words are solemnly significant. In these days when the discoveries of science have given us larger and larger conceptions of space, and of the mysterious powers which fill the universe everywhere, it becomes more than ever true that we never know how big a thing we are doing when we really pray "in the Name". We may not be able to understand, let alone explain, all the mystery of prayer; but we *do* know that God has chosen to work through the co-operating minds and wills and prayers of redeemed men and women, in the redeeming and blessing of others; and we *do* know that prayer opens up a channel for the release of divine grace and power which otherwise there would not be. Besides, what we call "mystery" in connection with prayer may only be our way of expressing ignorance of certain great laws, which, if we but knew them, would clear away all the mystery, and reveal the reason why prayer has such power.

Futhermore, we must ever remember that the prayer of redeemed and regenerated Christian believers is something which transcends both the mystery and the reality of so-called "natural law". When we pray in the name of Jesus we are on a *covenant* basis; and when we pray as regenerated "children of God" we are also on a *family* basis. The Scofield Bible has an excellent note on this:

"In the Sermon on the Mount Christ had announced the new basis of prayer, viz.: relationship (Matt. 6. vs. 9, 28–32). The believer is a child of God through the new birth (John 3. 3, note). The clear revelation of this fact at once establishes the reasonableness of prayer; a reasonableness against which the argument from the apparent uniformity of natural law shatters itself. God is more than a Creator, bringing a universe into being, and establishing laws for it; more than a decree-maker determining future events by an eternal fiat. Above all this is the divine family for whom the universe with its laws exists (Col. 1. 16–20; Heb. 1. 2; 2. 10, 11; Rom. 8. 17): 'When ye pray, say, Our Father.' What God habitually does in the material universe concerns the reverent investigator of that universe. What He may do in His own family concerns Him, and them, and is matter for divine promise and revelation. Science, which deals only with natural phenomena, cannot intrude there (I Cor. 2. 9)".

One thing we assuredly know, for we have proved it again and again, as also have millions of others: *IT WORKS*. When we have all had "our little say" about it, this remains true with comforting stolidity: *IT WORKS*. According to the materialistic scientist, natural laws explain everything; but in reality they do *not*; for they do not explain their own existence! The only explanation of laws is a Lawgiver who transcends them. That is why, whatever natural laws may be, men and women of prayer keep on finding that *IT WORKS*.

Not long ago, the heart-beat of a man in Mexico was listened to by his doctor who was in Spain! Much more, then, does not my omnipresent *divine* Father hear *my* heart-beats? A man nowadays may sit in a room in England, and type certain letters, making words and sentences, and even as he is doing it in England, the letters actually appear and spell themselves out until the message is complete away in Australia, at the very antipodes! Much more, then, do not my prayers spell themselves out at the throne of Him who *made* the subtle forces which men now harness to radio and television? Edward Young, the seventeenth-century poet, was abreast of all our twentieth-century knowledge when he wrote,

> Guard well thy thoughts;
> Thy thoughts are *heard* in heaven.

It has been aptly observed: "When we pray, we link ourselves with limitless love, and with the inexhaustible motive-power which spins the earth and controls the universe." Through prayer we ask and thereby appropriate an operation of that limitless love, wisdom, power in relation to our own needs and the needs of those for whom we intercede.

> The weary ones had rest,
> the sad ones joy,
> That day, and wondered "how".
> A ploughman, singing at his work
> had prayed,
> "Lord help them now."

Away in foreign lands,
    they wondered *"how"*
Their simple word had power ;
At home the Christians, two or three,
    had met
To pray an hour.

Yes, we are always wondering,
    wondering "how" ;
Because we do not see
Someone, unknown perhaps,
    and far away,
On bended knee.

There is a quite wonderful *reflexive* influence in prayer, by which we mean that it blesses not only the one prayed *for*, but the one who *prays*. How many Christians would find release from self-frustrations, inferiority complexes, oppressive moods, and subtle bondages, if only they would take up the ministry of intercession! It was such intercession which "turned the captivity" of the famous old patriarch, Job. In Job xlii. 10, we do *not* read, "And the Lord turned the captivity of Job when he prayed for *himself*." What we *do* find there is this: "And the Lord turned again the captivity of Job when he prayed *for his friends*." Such is the lovely "boomerang" effect of praying for others.

An outstanding medical man, Dr. Alexis Carrel says: "The influence of prayer on the human mind and body is as demonstrable as that of secreting glands. Its results can be measured in terms of increased physical buoyancy, greater intellectual vigour, moral stamina, and a deeper understanding of the realities underlying human relationships with God." Mark it well: that testimony is from an M.D., not a D.D.

If we prayed more, what transformations would there be in our own spirit and temper and character! It has been wittily remarked that "we never become backsliders on our knees", and that "he who kneels lowest rises highest", and that "he stands strongest who kneels longest". I myself have often noticed, both in myself and in others, that long lingerings in prayer ease tensions, refresh the mind, quieten the nerves, allay fear, renew courage, improve general health, smooth out cares, and take the weight out of worries. "Lord, teach us to pray!" (Luke xi. 1). "Lord, increase our faith!" (Luke xvii. 5). An old peasant was sitting alone in the last pew of the village church, when nearly all the other worshippers had left. "What are you waiting for?" he was asked. He replied, "I am just looking at *Him*, and *He* is looking at *me*." Even for our own sakes may the Lord teach us to linger more in prayer. How true are the oft-quoted lines of the late Archbishop Richard Chenevix Trench!—

> Lord, what a change within us one short hour
> Spent in Thy presence will avail to make!
> What heavy burdens from our bosoms take!
> What parched ground refresh as with a shower!
>
> We kneel, and all around us seems to lower;
> We rise, and all the distant and the near,
> Stands forth in sunny outline, brave and clear.
> We kneel, how weak! We rise, how full of power!
>
> Why therefore, should we do ourselves this wrong
> Or others—that we are not always strong—
> That we are sometimes overborne with care—
> That we should ever weak or heartless be,
> Anxious or troubled—when with us is prayer,
> And joy and strength and courage are with Thee?

This reflexive power of prayer, however, we have mentioned only incidentally. The main thought which we have in mind all through this present meditation is that prayer is the highest form of service. Prayer is the highest level of *missionary* service. Prayer is the highest level of *evangelistic* service. Prayer is the highest level of *pastoral* service. Prayer is the highest level of *deaconess* service. Prayer is the highest level of *teaching* service. Prayer is the highest level of *any* service. Yes, "Lord, teach us to pray!" Prayer is service—the highest service of all!

> When our God beholds us there,
> Wrestling in the place of prayer,
> Then the tide of battle turns,
> Then the flame of conquest burns;
> Then the faltering wail of fear
> Turns to victory's ringing cheer;
> Then the flag of truth prevails,
> Foes slink back and Satan quails.
> Bring us, Lord, oh, bring us there,
> Where we learn prevailing prayer.

POSTSCRIPT

"And this I pray, that your love may abound yet more and more, in knowledge and in all discernment."

—Phil. i. 9.

"There is no fear in love; but perfect love casteth out fear."—1 John iv. 18.

POSTSCRIPT

WE HAVE now traversed the three areas of this little book on knowing, and loving, and serving our Lord Jesus. There has been no attempt whatever at erudition, brilliance, or novelty, as will have been obvious; but we have kept ringing out from our belfry the three chimes which mean most of all to Christian hearts. As we said in our foreword, these are the "three aspects of our relationship with Christ which are continuingly fundamental, and indeed vital, to the spiritual life of the Christian believer": *KNOWING . . . LOVING . . . SERVING*. And now abide these three: knowing, loving, serving; but the greatest of these is *loving*. This brief postscript is to put a final emphasis there.

Lovest thou Me?

Three times our Lord asked Simon Peter: "Lovest thou Me?" Everything hinged on the answer to that. Everything hinges on *our* answer to it. Everything is determined by the degree to which we really love our Lord Jesus. The first thing which makes a true Christian minister or missionary or evangelist or preacher or Sunday school teacher, or leader or Christian worker of any kind, is not learning, not eloquence, not wisdom, not organising ability, not pleasing personality, not even a "passion for souls", but a love-passion for Jesus Himself. Nothing, *nothing, NOTHING,* can take the place of that. In the eyes of our heavenly Master, all else without that is like withered flowers. It comes before all else: *"Lovest* thou Me?"

"Feed My sheep."

The second thing which makes a true servant of the Lord is a sense of *ordination by Christ*. Three times our Lord responded to Peter's avowal of love. "Feed my lambs"; "Tend my sheep"; "Feed my sheep." Did you ever read Down in Water Street", the story of the Water Street Rescue Mission, New York? One night, years ago, there staggered into that mission a drunken criminal named Sam Hadley, who there and then became truly converted and morally revolutionised. Later, that same Sam Hadley became the leader of the Water Street Mission, where he did a simply amazing work for Christ. Hundreds of sotted drunkards and blackened criminals were saved and transformed; and when Sam Hadley died, he had one of the biggest funerals ever seen in America. Let me tell you what he says about his ordination to Christian service.

On the night when he was converted, he had just suffered his third bout of delirium tremens. He had one hundred and twenty-five forgeries against his name on one firm alone, and a list of crimes enough to put him in prison for the rest of his life. But at his conversion he became so wonderfully saved, that the very taste for drink and the lust for crime were plucked right out of his nature in one tremendous deliverance. That very night Christ gave him his commision to preach. Sam Hadley's own words shall tell it:

"I went out into the street, and looked up to the sky. I don't believe I had looked up for ten years. A drunken man never looks up; he always looks down. It was a glorious, star-lit night, and it seemed to me that I could see Jesus looking at me out of a million eyes. . . .

"That night, right on the corner of Broadway and Thirty-second Street, I was ordained to preach the everlasting Gospel, and have never doubted it for an instant. I have never stood before an audience without that vision inspiring me: 'If I can only make these people, dear Jesus, know who You are, they will love You too.' I have since been ordained by my beloved Methodist Episcopal Church, and I feel highly honoured; but I have always believed that I was ordained of *God* that night (i.e. that never-to-be-forgotten night under the stars)."

Oh, it is a great thing to have a sense of direct commission from Christ Himself, to have what I have heard called "the ordination of the pierced Hand". We should seek the realisation of it—and a waiting on Him in prayer will surely bring it, if we are in the line of His will.

"Follow Me."

The third thing which makes a true servant of our Lord is an obedient *following* of Him, just wherever He leads us. After our

Lord had asked Peter that question three times, "Lovest thou Me?" and had spoken that re-ordination three times, He added, "Follow Me". Peter then asked (and how Peter-like it was!) "Lord, what shall *this* man (i.e. John) do?"—to which our Lord replied, "What is that to thee? *Follow thou Me.*"

How meaningful it all seems!—three times, "Lovest thou Me?"; then three times a new ordination; then twice, *"Follow Me"*. Yes, this obedient following, prayerfully, willingly, lovingly, daily, is the third of these vital pre-requisites to true Christian service. It is the servant who thus "follows" who receives the daily anointing with heavenly unction, and is "endued with the power from on high" for special exploits. Closely following is not always easy. Sometimes it is hard indeed to the "flesh", for there are crucifixions for us in the wake of those beloved sandal-prints. But its rewards utterly outweigh all else; and the fellowship which it brings with our Lord is a sweet foretaste of heaven.

For many of us, this willingness to follow *utterly* is the centre-point, the sensitive nerve of our love to Christ. The "self" in us will yield up anything else—money, time, comforts, yes, *any*thing else if only it can dodge yielding up self-management and self-direction. There is no substitute, however, for this utter yielding and following, because there is no equivalent; nor is there anything which brings such a heartfelt realisation of oneness with our dear Lord.

"Wilt thou follow Me?" the Saviour asked.
  The road looked bright and fair,
And aflame with eager hope and zeal,
  I replied, "Yes, anywhere!"

"Wilt thou follow Me?" He later asked.
  The road grew dim ahead.
But I saw the love-glow in His face;
  "To the end, dear Lord," I said.

"Wilt thou follow Me?" I almost blanched,
  The road now fearsome grew;
But I felt His love-grip on my hand;
  And I answered, "Yes, right through."

"Dost thou follow still?" His tender tone,
  Mid the storm-clash thrilled my heart;
And I knew in a way before unknown,
  We should never, *never* part!

Well, there it is: "Lovest thou Me?" . . . "Feed my sheep" . . . "Follow Me." But "Lovest thou Me?" comes first, for it determines all else. When our love to Christ is what it should be, everything else falls into just its right place.

This is true in the matter of our *separation*. When we really love Him, do we allow worldly pleasures, unworthy practices, social compromises, in our lives? When we really love Him, as the first and dearest love of our hearts, does the renunciation of *any*thing unworthy or questionable greatly pain us? However hard any such renunciation may be to "the flesh", if our love to Christ is the supreme thing in us, it so over-rides "the flesh" as to make even the hard easy. To have to live the separated life because we *must*, as a Christian obligation, is always irksome; but to live the separated life because we *may*, as an expression of love to our heavenly Bridegroom, transforms duty into joyous privilege.

The same is true as regards our *consecration*. When we really love Him above all else, is there anything we would knowingly keep from Him? Could we ever say, "Lord Jesus, Son of God, who lovedst me, and gavest Thyself for me, I love Thee more than I love any other on earth or in heaven; but I am not prepared to give myself unreservedly to Thee"? Nay, is not our heart's language rather this?—

> In all my heart and will, O Jesus,
>   Be altogether King;
> Make me a loyal subject, Jesus,
>   To Thee, in everything.

And the same is true as regards our *sanctification*. Whatever may be our theory of sanctification or holiness, it is practically spurious unless it floods and sways the heart with love to *Him*. On the other hand, even though we know nothing of such theories as "eradication" or "counteraction", if our hearts love Him so dearly as to yield Him everything, then without a lot of so-called "claiming the blessing", He fills us with His sanctifying Holy Spirit; "perfect love casteth out fear" (1 John iv. 18); we are in the promised land, and we find ourselves singing:

> I've reached the land of corn and wine.
> Its riches all are freely mine!
> Here shines undimmed one blissful day,
> For all my night has passed away!

Oh, yes, our love to Him is the really determining thing. Let us pause to hear again His searching but heart-drawing question, deep in our consciousness: "Lovest thou Me?" Then let us linger again over the lovely mystery of *His* unquenchable, exquisite love for *us*. Then let us pray again with utter meaning,

> Break through my nature, mighty, heavenly love;
>   Clear every avenue of thought and brain.
> Flood my affections, purify my will;
>   Let nothing but Thine own pure life remain.
>
> Thus, wholly mastered, and by Thee possessed,
>   Forth from my life, spontaneous and free,
> Shall flow a stream of tenderness and grace,
>   Loving because *Thy* love now lives in *me*.

PPS. Yes, even a pps! As my mind now wanders back over the three areas of this little book, I find my thoughts framing themselves into a final hymn of longing. Perhaps it may express some other heart as well as my own.

> Oh, to know Him, deeply know Him,
>   Son of God, who died for me!
> Oh, to clasp Him, closely to clasp Him,
>   Though His form I cannot see!
> Oh, to see Him, inly see Him,
>   By an inwrought light divine,
> And, in ever-deepening union,
>   Daily, hourly prove Him mine!
>
> Oh, to love Him, dearly love Him,
>   With a heart for Him on fire!
> Oh, to show Him, really show Him,
>   He is my supreme desire!
> Oh, to prove Him, richly prove Him
>   With me, in me, tho' unseen,
> In a heart-to-heart communion,
>   Not a shade of doubt between!
>
> Oh, to serve Him, truly serve Him,
>   Living only in His will!
> Oh, to please Him, fully please Him,
>   All His purpose to fulfil!
> Thus to know and love and serve Him
>   Let my high absorption be,
> Finding, as His willing bondman,
>   Life, unfettered, radiant, free.